Developing Listening Comprehension for ESL Students

Developing Listening Comprehension for ESL Students

THE KINGDOM OF KOCHEN

Ted Plaister
University of Hawaii

Prentice-Hall, Inc., *Englewood Cliffs, New Jersey*

Library of Congress Cataloging in Publication Data

PLAISTER, TED.
   Developing listening comprehension for ESL students.

    1. English language—Textbooks for foreigners.
2. Listening—Study and teaching.   3. Note-taking.
I. Title.
PE1128.P55   428′ .2′4   75-25565
ISBN 0-13-204479-X

Printed in the United States of America

10   9

Prentice-Hall International, Inc., *London*
Prentice-Hall of Australia, Pty. Ltd., *Sydney*
Prentice-Hall of Canada, Ltd., *Toronto*
Prentice-Hall of India Private Limited, *New Delhi*
Prentice-Hall of Japan, Inc., *Tokyo*
Prentice-Hall of Southeast Asia (Pte.) Ltd., *Singapore*

To the students who taught me the most:

PRABHUNDHA VANASUPA
KENJI TSUCHISAWA

Contents

x   *Contents*

Acknowledgments

It is a pleasure to acknowledge the assistance which I received from Maureen O'Brien and Neal Scott, staff members of the English Language Institute, University of Hawaii, who taught the first version of this text and made many valuable contributions and suggestions. I am also grateful to Vincent Linares, who used the materials in a tutorial situation in Hawaii as well as with high school students in the Truk District of Micronesia. Thanks are also due to Janet Callender for using the materials with participants at the Japanese-American Institute of Management Sciences in Hawaii Kai.

I am indebted to the students of the English Language Institute, the students at Truk High School, and the participants in the JAIMS Program in Hawaii, all of whom were taught from various versions of these materials. Their interaction with the materials in classroom situations provided me with valuable feedback.

My thanks also to Marilyn Brauer, Carolyn Davidson, and Kathryn Woringer of Prentice-Hall, Inc. for their patience, good humor, and skill through all aspects of publication.

And to my students and friends, Dr. Prabhundha Vanasupa and Kenji Tsuchisawa, I am most deeply grateful, for it was they who provided the inspiration for the basic ideas in this text.

THE KINGDOM OF KOCHEN

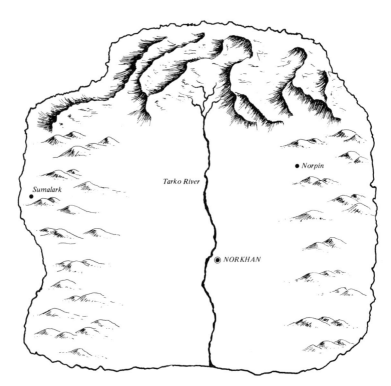

Area: *175,000 square miles*   Population: *25,000,000*

 Mountains   Foothills   Plains

Developing
Listening Comprehension
for ESL Students

Overview

READING PREPARATION

In this first lecture, the lecturer begins his discussion of the Kingdom of Kochen by asking his class how many have heard of the kingdom. It turns out that a few of them have. He says that he isn't surprised at this because names of countries around the world change constantly as a result of political problems, governments being toppled, the rise of nationalistic feelings, etc.

Then he locates Kochen on the map so that the students can visualize where it is. He points out that Kochen is in the middle of Southeast Asia. Kochen is not very big—approximately 175,000 square miles. Thailand is a little larger, having about 200,000 square miles.

The lecturer says that he will not be giving a lot of detailed information about Kochen's geography, but rather will be giving the listener a general picture. The main feature of Kochen is that it is rather flat. It does have some small mountains, but these are only about 5,000 feet high. Kochen has four regions. One, the central plain area, is a very fertile part of the country. Kochen grows its rice—the staple food—in this plain. The Tarko River flows through this plain. This river begins in the mountains of the north. The central plain is roughly a square with the river flowing through its center. In the north, there are mountains and the soils are of poor quality. Bordering the central plain are the east and west regions. These are made up of rolling foothills and their soil is reasonably good. He concludes this part of the lecture by mentioning that the east and west regions are next in importance in food production after the central plain.

He finishes the lecture by restating that there are four regions in the country: one with mountains, two with foothills, and central plain with a river traversing it.

DICTATION

1. _____	1. _____
2. _____	2. _____
3. _____	3. _____
4. _____	4. _____
5. _____	5. _____
6. _____	6. _____
7. _____	7. _____
8. _____	8. _____
9. _____	9. _____
10. _____	10. _____
11. _____	11. _____
12. _____	12. _____
13. _____	13. _____
14. _____	14. _____
15. _____	15. _____
16. _____	16. _____
17. _____	17. _____
18. _____	18. _____
19. _____	19. _____
20. _____	20. _____
21. _____	21. _____

22. _____ 22. _____

23. _____ 23. _____

24. _____ 24. _____

25. _____ 25. _____

Number correct _____

AUDING PROMPT A

I'd like to begin our discussion of the Kingdom of Kochen by asking how many of you have heard of Kochen. I see. Well, at least a handful of you have heard of the place. I'm really not overly surprised by this because, after all, names of countries around the globe keep changing all the time as political problems arise, governments are overthrown, nationalism rises, and so forth.

We'd better locate Kochen on the map, I guess, so that you have a picture in your mind of where it is. As you can see from the map, it is located right here in the middle of Southeast Asia. It's not a very big country in terms of size. The land area is approximately 175,000 square miles, which makes it a little smaller than Thailand, which has a land area of some 200,000 square miles.

I don't want to give you too much detailed information about the geography of Kochen, but I think you should have a general picture of what it's like. Primarily Kochen is rather flat. There are some small mountains, but nothing much over about 5,000 feet. Geographically speaking, there are four regions in Kochen. There is the central plain area which is the most fertile part of the country. It is in this central plain area that the bulk of Kochen's staple food—rice—is grown. This plain is watered by the Tarko River, which arises in the northern part of the kingdom. The central plain is sort of block-shaped and the Tarko River cuts straight through it. The northern region is somewhat mountainous and the soils aren't very good. On either side of the central plain are the east and west regions, which are composed mainly of rolling foothills with fairly good soil. These two parts of the country are next in importance as far as food production goes, but I am getting a little ahead of myself.

So there are four regions—one mountainous, two with rolling foothills, and a fertile central plain cut through by a major waterway.

AUDING PROMPT B

_____ _____ _____ begin _____ discussion of _____ Kingdom of Kochen _____ asking how many _____ _____ have heard of Kochen. _____ _____. _____, _____ _____ _____ handful of you have heard of _____ place. I'm _____ not _____ surprised _____ _____ because, _____ _____, names of countries _____ _____ _____ keep changing _____ _____ _____ as political problems arise, governments are overthrown, nationalism rises, _____ _____ _____.

_____ _____ locate Kochen on _____ map, _____ _____, so _____ you have a picture in _____ mind _____ where it is. _____ you can see from _____ map, _____ _____ located right _____ in _____ middle of Southeast Asia. _____ not _____ very big country _____ _____ _____ size. _____ _____ area is approximately 175,000 square miles, _____ _____ _____ a little smaller than Thailand, which has _____ _____ area of some 200,000 square miles.

_____ don't want to give _____ too much detailed information about _____

geography of Kochen, but ____ ____ you should have a general picture ____
____ ____ ____. ____ Kochen is rather flat. ____ ____ some small mountains, ____ nothing much over ____ 5,000 feet. Geographically ____, ____
____ four regions in Kochen. ____ ____ ____ central plain area which is
____ most fertile part ____ ____ ____. ____ ____ in ____ central plain
area ____ ____ bulk of Kochen's staple food—rice—is grown. ____ plain is
watered by ____ Tarko River, which arises in ____ northern part ____ ____
____. ____ central plain is ____ ____ block-shaped and ____ Tarko River
cuts straight through it. ____ northern region is ____ mountainous and ____
soils aren't ____ good. On either side of ____ central plain are ____ east and
west regions, ____ ____ composed mainly of rolling foothills with fairly good
soil. These two parts of ____ country ____ next in importance as far as food
production goes, ____ ____ ____ ____ ____ ____ ____ ____ ____.

____ there are four regions—one mountainous, two with somewhat rolling
foothills, and ____ fertile central plain cut through by ____ major waterway.

AUDING PROMPT C

—— begin —— discussion —— Kochen —— how many —— heard ——
Kochen ——. —— handful —— heard —— place ——. —— not —— surprised —— names —— countries —— changing —— political —— problems
—— governments —— overthrown —— nationalism ——.

—— locate —— Kochen —— map —— picture —— mind ——. —— see
—— map —— located —— middle —— Southeast Asia ——. —— not ——
big —— country ——. —— area —— approximately —— 175,000 —— smaller —— Thailand —— area —— 200,000 ——.

—— don't —— give —— detailed —— information —— about —— geography —— should —— have —— general —— picture ——. —— Kochen
—— flat ——. —— small —— mountains —— 5,000 ——. —— geographically —— four —— regions ——. —— central —— plain —— most —— fertile ——. —— central —— plain —— bulk —— staple —— rice —— grown
——. —— plain —— watered —— Tarko River —— arises —— northern
——. —— central —— plain —— block-shaped —— River —— straight ——
through ——. —— northern —— region —— mountainous —— soils ——
aren't —— good ——. —— either —— side —— east —— west —— regions
—— composed —— mainly —— rolling —— foothills —— fairly —— good
—— soil ——. —— two —— parts —— country —— next —— importance
—— food —— production ——.

—— four —— regions —— mountainous —— two —— rolling —— foothills —— fertile —— central —— plain —— cut —— through —— major
—— waterway ——.

NOTES

Kochen

    Location—middle of S.E. Asia

    Small country, 175,000 sq. mi. (Thailand—200,000 sq. mi.)

    Geography

        Rather flat, some small mtns (about 5,000 ft. maximum)

        4 regions

            Central plain, most fertile, rice (staple) grown here

                Watered by Tarko River—comes from north

                Block-shaped, T. River cuts through

            Northern region

                Somewhat mountainous, soils not very good

            East and West regions—on either side of central plain

                Rolling foothills

                Fairly good soil

                Next in importance (to central pl.) for food prodn.

YOUR NOTES

QUIZ

Instructions: Answer the Quiz after studying the *notes* you have taken from the lecture.

1. Where is the Kingdom of Kochen?

2. What is the approximate land area of Kochen in square miles?
   ( ) 200,000
   ( ) 175,000
   ( ) 150,000

3. Describe the *main* geographical features of Kochen.

4. How many geographic regions does Kochen have?

5. Where does Kochen grow its rice?

6. What is the source of the water to irrigate the rice crop?

7. Rank the regions of Kochen with respect to food production from best to poorest.

QUIZ ANSWERS

1. Where is the Kingdom of Kochen?
   Middle of Southeast Asia.

2. What is the approximate land area of Kochen in square miles?
   ( ) 200,000
   (X) 175,000
   ( ) 150,000

3. Describe the *main* geographical features of Kochen.
   It's rather flat. There are some small mountains, about 5,000 feet. There are rolling foothills.

4. How many geographic regions does Kochen have?
   Four.

5. Where does Kochen grow its rice?
   Central plain.

6. What is the source of the water to irrigate the rice crop?
   Tarko River.

7. Rank the regions of Kochen with respect to food production from best to poorest.
   1. Central Plain
   2. East and West Regions
   3. Northern Region

Climate

READING PREPARATION

The lecturer says that he wants to take a look in this lecture at the general weather picture in Kochen. He says that there is a relationship between this and what the Kochenese do for their livelihood, the kind of things they grow, etc.

In common with the whole region, Kochen has a monsoon kind of climate: it is a wet tropical area. He defines the word *monsoon* as meaning a wind system which influences large climatic regions and changes its direction during different seasons. He notes that the word is from an Arabic word which means season. Clouds and heavy rains are brought in by the hot, wet southwest monsoon wind. In contrast to this are the northeast monsoons, which carry warm, dry air from China with resulting clear skies. From November to February is the warm, dry season while from May to October is the rainy season. There is a transition period—March and April—which is rather warm. Thus there are three distinct seasons, one of which is short. The lecturer names the seasons the dry, rainy, and hot seasons. He suggests that this pattern of weather is typical of the entire area, and similar to that which is found in Thailand.

The lecturer asks what the real temperatures are like. His first example is the lowest temperature on record: 55 degrees Fahrenheit. However, he says, temperatures during the coldest part of the dry season generally are in the neighborhood of 60 to 65 degrees Fahrenheit. At the opposite end of the scale, the hottest temperature on record is 105 degrees Fahrenheit. The average temperature is about 100 during the warmest part of the hot season. The point is made that four or five days of 100-degree weather can make a person uncomfortable, and anyone who has been through something like this is quick to realize it. This is especially true with high humidity. He then runs out of time.

DICTATION

1. _____	1. _____
2. _____	2. _____
3. _____	3. _____
4. _____	4. _____
5. _____	5. _____
6. _____	6. _____
7. _____	7. _____
8. _____	8. _____
9. _____	9. _____
10. _____	10. _____
11. _____	11. _____
12. _____	12. _____
13. _____	13. _____
14. _____	14. _____
15. _____	15. _____
16. _____	16. _____
17. _____	17. _____
18. _____	18. _____
19. _____	19. _____
20. _____	20. _____
21. _____	21. _____

22. _____   22. _____

23. _____   23. _____

24. _____   24. _____

25. _____   25. _____

Number correct _____

AUDING PROMPT A

Today I'd like to take a look at the general weather picture in Kochen. This ties in with what the Kochenese do for a living, what kind of crops they grow, and things like that.

Like the whole area, Kochen has a monsoon type of climate. So it is a wet tropical region. The word *monsoon* is from an Arabic word meaning season and refers to a wind system that influences large climatic regions and changes its direction seasonally. In Kochen there are hot, wet southwest monsoon winds which bring in the clouds and heavy rains. Then there are the northeast monsoons which carry warm, dry air from China, which results in clear skies. The warm, dry season runs from November to February and the rainy season is from May to October. Things really begin to warm up in March and April, which is sort of a transition period. So we have three distinct seasons, one of them rather short. To give these seasons a handle, let's call them the dry season, the rainy season, and the hot season. Again, this is pretty typical of this whole area and certainly follows the pattern we find in Thailand, for example.

What are the actual temperatures like? The lowest recorded temperature is 55 degrees Fahrenheit, but temperatures during the coldest part of the dry season usually run around 60 to 65 degrees Fahrenheit. At the other end of the scale, the highest temperature ever recorded was 105 degrees Fahrenheit and again this is somewhat extreme. Usually the mercury hits about 100 during the hottest part of the hot season. But, as those of you know who have experienced weather like this, if you get a stretch of four or five days of 100-degree weather you can be pretty miserable. This is especially true if the humidity happens to take a jump. I guess that's all we have time for.

AUDING PROMPT B

_____ _____ _____ _____ _____ _____ look at _____ _____ weather _____ in Kochen. _____ ties in with what _____ Kochenese do for _____ living, _____ kind of crops they grow, _____ _____ _____ _____.

Like _____ whole area, Kochen has _____ monsoon _____ _____ climate. _____ _____ _____ _____ wet tropical region. _____ _____ *monsoon* _____ from _____ Arabic word meaning season _____ refers to _____ wind system _____ influences large climatic regions _____ changes _____ direction seasonally. _____ Kochen _____ _____ hot, wet southwest monsoon winds _____ bring in _____ clouds _____ heavy rains. _____ _____ _____ _____ northeast monsoons _____ carry warm, dry air from China, _____ results in clear skies. _____ warm, dry season runs _____ November to February _____ _____ rainy season is _____ May to October. Things _____ _____ _____ warm up in March and April, _____ is sort of _____ transition period. _____ _____ _____ three distinct seasons, one _____ _____ rather short. _____ _____ _____ _____ _____ _____, _____ call

them _____ dry season, _____ rainy season, _____ _____ hot season. _____,
_____ _____ pretty typical of _____ whole area _____ _____ follows _____ pattern we find in Thailand, _____ _____ .

What are _____ actual temperatures _____? _____ lowest recorded _____ is
55 degrees Fahrenheit, _____ temperatures during _____ coldest part of _____
dry season usually _____ around 60 to 65 degrees Fahrenheit. _____ _____ other
end of _____ scale, _____ highest temperature _____ recorded _____ 105 degrees Fahrenheit _____ _____ this is _____ extreme. Usually _____ _____ _____
about 100 during _____ hottest part _____ _____ _____ _____ . _____, _____
_____ _____ _____ _____ _____ _____ _____ _____ _____ _____ , _____ _____
_____ _____ _____ _____ _____ _____ _____ _____ _____ _____ -_____ _____
_____ _____ _____ _____ _____ . _____ _____ _____ _____ _____ _____ _____
_____ _____ _____ _____ _____ . _____ _____ that's all we have time for.

AUDING PROMPT C

—— weather —— Kochen ——. —— ties in —— Kochenese —— living ——
crops ——.

—— Kochen —— monsoon —— climate ——. —— wet —— tropical ——
region ——. —— *monsoon* —— Arabic —— meaning —— season —— refers
—— wind —— system —— influences —— climatic —— regions ——
changes —— direction —— seasonally ——. —— Kochen —— hot —— wet
—— southwest —— monsoon —— bring —— clouds —— heavy —— rains
——. —— northeast —— monsoons —— carry —— warm —— dry —— air
—— China —— results —— clear —— skies ——. —— warm —— dry ——
season —— November —— February —— rainy —— season —— May ——
October ——. —— warm —— March —— April —— transition —— period
——. —— three —— distinct —— seasons ——. —— dry season —— rainy
season —— hot season ——. —— typical —— area —— follows —— pattern
—— Thailand ——.

—— actual —— temperatures ——? —— lowest —— 55 degrees ——
Fahrenheit —— temperatures —— during —— coldest —— part —— dry season —— usually —— 60 —— 65 —— degrees —— Fahrenheit ——. ——
other —— end —— scale —— highest —— temperature —— recorded ——
105 degrees —— Fahrenheit ——. —— usually —— 100 —— during ——
hottest —— part ——. —— that's —— all ——.

NOTES

Weather—Kochen

    Re living, crops

Kochen—monsoon type climate

    Wet trop. region

    Monsoon (Arabic word) = season

    Wind system influences large climatic regions, changes directions seasonally

    Hot wet SW mons. winds bring clouds/heavy rains

    NE mons. carry warm dry air fr. China = clear skies

Warm dry season—Nov to Feb

Rainy season—May to Oct

Mar/April = transition period (hot)

Dry, rainy, hot seasons—typical of whole area

Lowest temp—55° F, avg. 60–65°

Highest temp—105°, avg. 100° hottest part

YOUR NOTES

QUIZ

Instructions: Answer the Quiz after studying the *notes* you have taken from the lecture.

1. What *type* of climate does Kochen have?

2. How would you describe the climate for the general region in which Kochen is located?
   ( ) Dry tropical
   ( ) Moist semi-tropical
   ( ) Wet tropical

3. What are the three seasons in Kochen?

   1. _____

   2. _____

   3. _____

4. What are the dates (in months) of the three seasons listed in 3, above?

   1. _____ to _____

   2. _____ to _____

   3. _____ to _____

5. What are the approximate temperature ranges in Kochen (in Fahrenheit)?

QUIZ ANSWERS

1. What *type* of climate does Kochen have?
   Monsoon

2. How would you describe the climate for the general region in which Kochen is located?
   ( ) Dry tropical
   ( ) Moist semi-tropical
   (X) Wet tropical

3. What are the three seasons in Kochen?
   1. Dry
   2. Hot
   3. Rainy

4. What are the dates (in months) of the three seasons listed in 3, above?
   1. November to February
   2. March to April
   3. May to October

5. What are the approximate temperature ranges in Kochen (in Fahrenheit)?
   55 to 105

Agriculture (I)

READING PREPARATION

The lecturer begins by saying that the kingdom of Kochen is predominantly an agricultural country. He quotes figures which show that some 85 percent of its people are engaged in farming. Of the 85 percent who are in farming, 90 percent are in the rice-growing business. He locates Kochen as being in the middle of the Southeast Asian rice belt and notes that the countries which border on Kochen also grow rice.

The lecturer continues that approximately 75 percent of the land which is cultivated in Kochen is used for raising rice. Further, the Kochenese export a rather significant amount of rice. Other crops which are grown by the Kochenese are of little significance economically, and are sold for domestic use. The lecturer explains that the Kochenese grow the *Indica*—the long-grain rice—rather than the *Japonica*—the short-grain rice. Touching upon rice yields, he mentions that they are very good because of the good natural conditions and also because the Kochenese government has spent a lot of money on developing agriculture. Natural rainfall is used to grow rice, but irrigation has also been developed so that areas which would have low yields of rice if farmed under natural rainfall now are productive to an economically significant degree. There is a good agricultural extension service, according to the lecturer. And he makes the point that there is a combination of the natural resources which are good, and the good farming practices which are fostered by agents of the agricultural extension service. All of these things add up, he says, to some of the best yields of good-quality rice anywhere in the world.

DICTATION

1. _____	1. _____
2. _____	2. _____
3. _____	3. _____
4. _____	4. _____
5. _____	5. _____
6. _____	6. _____
7. _____	7. _____
8. _____	8. _____
9. _____	9. _____
10. _____	10. _____
11. _____	11. _____
12. _____	12. _____
13. _____	13. _____
14. _____	14. _____
15. _____	15. _____
16. _____	16. _____
17. _____	17. _____
18. _____	18. _____
19. _____	19. _____
20. _____	20. _____
21. _____	21. _____

22. _____   22. _____

23. _____   23. _____

24. _____   24. _____

25. _____   25. _____

Number correct _____

AUDING PROMPT A

Kochen is predominantly an agricultural country and the latest figures that I could get my hands on indicate that approximately 85 percent of the people are farmers of one kind or another. And of this 85 percent of the people who make their living by farming, 90 percent are rice farmers. All the neighboring countries in this area are also rice producers, so Kochen is sitting right in the middle of the Southeast Asian rice belt.

Of the cultivated land in Kochen, about 75 percent is devoted to rice cultivation. Of economic importance is the fact that the Kochenese export a fair amount of rice. I won't go into that here, but will touch on it a bit later. The other agricultural crops which are grown in Kochen are not of economic significance. These crops are all consumed in the domestic market. The Kochenese, for the most part, grow only the long-grain rice, the *Indica* type. For those of you who know nothing about rice culture, there are two major types of rice: *Japonica* and *Indica*. The *Japonica* is the so-called short-grain rice favored by the Japanese and others. Rice yields are extremely good in Kochen not only because of extremely favorable natural conditions, but also because the government of Kochen has poured a lot of money into agricultural development. Not only is the natural rainfall used to grow rice, but there is also an extensive irrigation system which has been developed by the Ministry of Agriculture to bring marginal areas into production. The Kochenese have a rather good agricultural extension service which assists farmers in solving their agricultural problems. So what we have here is a combination of good natural resources plus advanced cultural practices enhanced by an aggressive and well-trained group of agricultural extension agents. The results speak for themselves: one of the highest yields of excellent-quality rice in the world.

That's all I want to cover today. I'll be continuing with agriculture next time.

AUDING PROMPT B

Kochen is predominantly _____ agricultural country _____ _____ latest figures _____ _____ _____ _____ _____ _____ _____ indicate _____ approximately 85 percent of _____ people are farmers _____ _____ _____ _____ _____. _____ of this 85 percent _____ _____ _____ _____ _____ _____ _____ _____ _____, 90 percent are rice farmers. All _____ neighboring countries _____ _____ _____ are _____ rice producers, so Kochen _____ sitting _____ in _____ middle of _____ Southeast Asian rice belt.

Of _____ cultivated land in Kochen, about 75 percent _____ devoted to rice _____. _____ economic importance is _____ fact that _____ Kochenese export _____ fair amount of rice. _____ won't go into that here, _____ _____ touch on it _____ _____ later. _____ other agricultural crops _____ _____ grown in Kochen _____ not of economic significance. These _____ _____ all consumed in _____ domestic market. _____ Kochenese, for the most part, grow _____ _____ long-

grain rice, ____ *Indica* type. ____ ____ ____ ____ ____ ____ ____
____ ____ ____, there are two major types of rice: *Japonica* and *Indica*.
____ *Japonica* is ____ ____ short-grain rice favored by ____ Japanese and
others. Rice yields ____ extremely good in Kochen ____ ____ because of extremely favorable natural conditions, ____ also because ____ government of
Kochen has poured a lot of money into agricultural development. Not only
____ ____ natural rainfall ____ to grow rice, but ____ ____ also ____ ex-
tensive irrigation system ____ ____ ____ developed by ____ Ministry of
Agriculture to bring marginal areas into production. ____ Kochenese have
____ rather good agricultural extension service ____ assists farmers ____
solving ____ agricultural problems. ____ ____ ____ have ____ ____
____ combination of good natural resources plus advanced cultural practices
enhanced by ____ aggressive ____ well-trained ____ ____ agricultural extension agents. ____ results speak for themselves: one of ____ highest yields
of excellent quality rice in ____ world.
    That's all ____ ____ ____ ____ ____. ____ ____ continuing with ag-
riculture next time.

AUDING PROMPT C

—— Kochen —— predominantly —— agricultural —— latest —— figures
—— indicate —— approximately —— 85 percent —— people —— farmers
——. —— of —— 85 percent —— 90 percent —— rice farmers ——. ——
All —— neighboring —— countries —— rice —— producers —— Kochen
—— middle —— Southeast Asian —— rice —— belt ——.
    —— cultivated —— land —— Kochen —— 75 percent —— devoted ——
rice ——. —— economic —— importance —— fact —— Kochenese —— export —— fair —— amount —— rice ——. —— other —— agricultural ——
crops —— Kochen —— not —— economic —— significance ——. —— consumed —— domestic —— market ——. —— Kochenese —— grow ——
long-grain —— rice —— *Indica* —— major —— types —— *Japonica* ——
Indica ——. —— *Japonica* —— short-grain —— favored —— Japanese
——. —— rice —— yields —— extremely —— good —— Kochen —— because —— extremely —— favorable —— natural —— conditions —— also
—— because —— government —— Kochen —— poured —— lot —— money
—— agricultural —— development ——. —— not —— only —— rainfall
—— grow —— rice —— also —— extensive —— irrigation —— system ——
developed —— Ministry —— Agriculture —— bring —— marginal —— areas
—— production ——. —— Kochenese —— good —— agricultural —— extension —— service —— assists —— farmers —— solving —— problems
——. —— combination —— natural —— resources —— advanced —— cultural —— practices —— enhanced —— aggressive —— agricultural —— extension —— agents——. —— highest —— yields —— excellent —— quality
—— rice ——.

NOTES

Kochen

> Predominantly agric. country
>
> 85% of people are farmers—90% of these grow rice
>
> In middle of SEA rice belt
>
> 75% of land (cultivated) in rice
>
> > Export fair amt. of rice
>
> Other agric. crops of no economic significance—consumed at home
>
> Rice—
>
> > Kochenese grow Indica (long-grain)
> >
> > Yields very good
> >
> > > Extremely favorable natural conditions
> > >
> > > Gov't has pushed development
> > >
> > > Good irrigation system—dev. by Min of Agric (brings marginal land into
> > >
> > > > prodn)
> > >
> > > Good agric. ext. service
> >
> > Summary—
> >
> > > Good natural resources + good cultural practices + good ext. agents =
> > >
> > > > one of highest yields of quality rice in world

YOUR NOTES

QUIZ

1. What percentage of the people in Kochen are rice farmers?
   ( ) 85
   ( ) 90
   ( ) 76.5

2. Of all the cultivated land in Kochen, what percent is NOT devoted to rice?
   ( ) 25
   ( ) 75
   ( ) 50

3. How much rice does Kochen normally export?
   ( ) a small amount
   ( ) a fair amount
   ( ) a large amount

4. Of what economic significance are the agricultural crops other than rice which are grown in Kochen?
   ( ) practically none
   ( ) some
   ( ) a fair amount
   ( ) a great deal

5. Which type of rice do the Kochenese grow?
   ( ) Japonica
   ( ) Indica
   ( ) Both Japonica and Indica

6. Characterize the natural conditions for growing rice in Kochen.

7. Explain the role of the Ministry of Agriculture in promoting rice culture in Kochen.

QUIZ ANSWERS

1. What percentage of the people in Kochen are rice farmers?
   - ( ) 85
   - ( ) 90
   - (X) 76.5

2. Of all the cultivated land in Kochen, what percent is NOT devoted to rice?
   - (X) 25
   - ( ) 75
   - ( ) 50

3. How much rice does Kochen normally export?
   - ( ) a small amount
   - (X) a fair amount
   - ( ) a large amount

4. Of what economic significance are the agricultural crops other than rice which are grown in Kochen?
   - (X) practically none
   - ( ) some
   - ( ) a fair amount
   - ( ) a great deal

5. Which type of rice do the Kochenese grow?
   - ( ) Japonica
   - (X) Indica
   - ( ) Both Japonica and Indica

6. Characterize the natural conditions for growing rice in Kochen.
   Extremely good (or Very good or Very favorable or Excellent)

7. Explain the role of the Ministry of Agriculture in promoting rice culture in Kochen.
   It has put a lot of money into agricultural development. An extensive irrigation system has been developed, and the agricultural extension service is well-trained.

Agriculture (II)

READING PREPARATION

The lecturer asks you to recall that he mentioned rice as being the basic, most important crop in Kochen. He reminds you that he said that the other crops grown there are not of economic importance; that is, they are not exported to other countries. He says that these crops other than rice are certainly of *some* importance economically because they add to the income of the farmers who grow them. He then talks about what these crops are.

The first he mentions is corn. According to the lecture, the main use of corn is as food for livestock, chickens, geese, and ducks. Some sweet corn is also grown in the country, but it is for a special kind of market. Other crops he mentions are peanuts and soya beans.

The next crop he considers is sugar cane. He notes that about a third of the country's requirement is grown. He mentions in passing that sugar cane is eaten as a confection in its raw state. He tells about the use of sugar from palm trees as a sweetener.

He moves on to discuss the coconut, which he says grows throughout this general area, but is used at home rather than being grown for export as it is in the Philippines. The Kochenese, he says, eat a lot of fresh coconut in a variety of forms. He adds a personal note, telling of a dessert like a custard which he once enjoyed there.

The next topic mentioned is vegetables, which are grown mostly for the local market. These vegetables are green, leafy vegetables, for example, cabbage and lettuce.

Last, he mentions that Kochen is a virtual paradise when it comes to fruit. He places Indonesia at the head of the list of fruit-growing countries, but adds that Kochen has many kinds in good supply. He closes by saying that Kochen has many varieties of bananas. He then runs out of time and stops.

DICTATION

1. _____   1. _____

2. _____   2. _____

3. _____   3. _____

4. _____   4. _____

5. _____   5. _____

6. _____   6. _____

7. _____   7. _____

8. _____   8. _____

9. _____   9. _____

10. _____   10. _____

11. _____   11. _____

12. _____   12. _____

13. _____   13. _____

14. _____   14. _____

15. _____   15. _____

16. _____   16. _____

17. _____   17. _____

18. _____   18. _____

19. _____   19. _____

20. _____   20. _____

21. _____   21. _____

22. _____ _____   22. _____

23. _____ _____   23. _____

24. _____ _____   24. _____

25. _____ _____   25. _____

Number correct _____

AUDING PROMPT A

You will recall that I mentioned rice as being the number one crop in Kochen. I also said that the other crops were not of economic importance and I meant by this, of course, that these crops were not exported. Certainly these crops are of economic importance in that they contribute to the income of the farmers who produce them. Let's take a look at what some of them are.

A fair amount of corn is grown. This corn is used primarily as a feed grain for livestock and poultry. A small amount of sweet corn is grown, but this is mostly for specialty markets. Other crops along this line are peanuts and soya beans.

There is a pretty good acreage of sugar cane grown, but only enough to supply about a third of the country's needs. Sugar cane, incidentally, is eaten in its raw state as a kind of confection. Another sweetening agent is palm sugar, its source being a type of palm tree.

All throughout this area you will find the coconut. Again, the coconut is pretty much used for domestic consumption with practically no exporting of copra such as we would find from the Philippines, for example. A lot of fresh coconut is eaten in various forms. Once when I was in Kochen, I had a delicious dessert—a custardlike dessert—made with coconuts.

A variety of vegetables is grown, but again these vegetables are for the local market. Many of these are the green, leafy type of vegetable such as cabbage and lettuce. There are many, many of these.

When it comes to fruit, Kochen is a real paradise. Now, I suppose that of all places on the globe, maybe Indonesia may have more and different fruits, more varieties of fruits than any other place. Yet, I must say, Kochen certainly has an ample supply of many different kinds. In this part of the world, you would expect to find bananas and Kochen has more than its share of different kinds. I see our time is up, so I'll stop at this point.

AUDING PROMPT B

_____ _____ recall _____ I mentioned rice _____ being _____ number one crop in Kochen. _____ also _____ _____ _____ other crops _____ not of economic importance _____ I meant _____ _____ , _____ _____ , _____ these crops _____ not exported. _____ these crops _____ of economic importance _____ _____ they contribute to _____ income of _____ farmers who produce them. Let's _____ _____ look at _____ some _____ _____ _____ .

_____ fair amount _____ corn _____ grown. _____ corn _____ used primarily as _____ feed grain for livestock _____ poultry. _____ small amount _____ sweet corn _____ grown, _____ _____ _____ mostly for specialty markets. Other crops _____ _____ _____ are peanuts _____ soya beans.

_____ _____ _____ pretty good acreage of sugar cane _____ , _____ only enough to supply about _____ third of _____ country's needs. Sugar cane, _____ , _____ eaten in _____ raw state as _____ _____ _____ confection. Another sweetening ___ ___ palm sugar, ___ source ___ type of palm tree.

All throughout ___ area ___ ___ find ___ coconut. ___, ___ coconut ___ pretty much used for domestic consumption ___ practically no exporting of copra ___ as we ___ find from ___ Philippines, ___ ___. ___ lot of fresh coconut ___ eaten ___ ___ ___. ___ ___ ___ ___ ___ ___, ___ ___ ___ ___ ___ ___—___ ___ ___—___ ___ ___.

___ variety of vegetables ___ grown, ___ ___ ___ vegetables are for ___ local market. Many ___ ___ are ___ green, leafy type ___ ___ such as cabbage ___ lettuce. ___ ___ ___, many of these.

When it comes to fruit, Kochen is ___ ___ paradise. ___, ___ ___ ___ of all places on ___ globe, Indonesia may have more ___ different fruits, more varieties ___ ___ than any other ___. ___, ___ ___ ___, Kochen ___ has ___ ample supply of ___ different kinds. In this part of ___ world, ___ ___ expect to find bananas ___ Kochen has more than its share ___ different kinds. ___ ___ ___ time is up, ___ ___ ___ ___ ___ ___.

AUDING PROMPT C

— recall — rice — number — one — crop — Kochen —. — other — crops — not — economic — importance — meant — crops — not — exported —. — crops — economic — importance — contribute — income — farmers —.

— fair — amount — corn — grown —. — corn — used — primarily — feed — livestock — poultry —. — small — amount — sweet — corn — grown — mostly — specialty — markets —. — other — crops — peanuts — soya beans —.

— good — acreage — sugar cane — enough — supply — about — third — country's — needs —. — Sugar cane — eaten — raw — state — confection —. — another — sweeting — palm — sugar — source — type — palm — tree —.

— throughout — area — coconut —. — coconut — used — domestic — consumption — practically — no — exporting — copra — find — Philippines —. — lot — fresh — coconut — eaten —.

— variety — vegetables — for — local — market —. — many — green — leafy — type — cabbage — lettuce —.

— fruit — Kochen — paradise —. — on globe — Indonesia — more — different — fruits — more — varieties —. — Kochen — ample — supply — different — kinds —. — part — world — expect — find — bananas — Kochen — share — different — kinds —.

NOTES

Rice—#1 crop in K.

  Other crops not exported

      ‖   contribute income to farmers

Corn

  Used as feed for livestock, poultry

  Sweet corn—for specialty mkts.

Peanuts, soya beans (same as corn)

Sugar cane

  1/3 of needs

  Used as confection

Palm sugar (from palm trees)

Coconut

  Home use

  No copra exp.

  Fresh coconut eaten

Vegs

  Green leafy types, many (ex. cabbage, lettuce, etc.)

Fruit

  Many varieties, Indonesia considered tops

  Bananas, many kinds

YOUR NOTES

QUIZ

1. What is the principal crop of Kochen?

2. What is the main use for the corn grown in Kochen?

3. What fraction of Kochen's sugar requirements is met locally?
   ( ) One-half
   ( ) Two-thirds
   ( ) One-third

4. How is the coconut mainly utilized in Kochen?
   ( ) Exported as copra
   ( ) Eaten as dessert
   ( ) Consumed fresh

5. How would you characterize the vegetables grown in Kochen

6. What did the lecturer say about the fruits of Kochen?

QUIZ ANSWERS

1. What is the principal crop of Kochen?
   Rice

2. What is the main use for the corn grown in Kochen?
   Feed grain for livestock and poultry. (Or) Livestock and poultry feed.

3. What fraction of Kochen's sugar requirements is met locally?
   ( ) One-half
   ( ) Two-thirds
   (X) One-third

4. How is the coconut mainly utilized in Kochen?
   ( ) Exported as copra
   ( ) Eaten as dessert
   (X) Consumed fresh

5. How would you characterize the vegetables grown in Kochen?
   Green leafy types

6. What did the lecturer say about the fruits of Kochen?
   Tremendous variety; lots of different kinds of bananas.

Principal Cities

READING PREPARATION

The lecturer now discusses the centers of population in the Kingdom of Kochen. Thus, he changes the topic from agriculture, but says that he will return to agriculture if there is time.

He starts with the capital city of Norkhan and mentions that it has a population of approximately 5,000,000 people. This makes it the largest city in Kochen. Norpin is the second largest city, with 1,500,000. The third big city is Sumalark, which has a population of about 1,000,000. Therefore, in the three principal cities there is a total population of 7,500,000. The lecturer says that the total population of Kochen is 25,000,000 according to data from the census taken in 1975. He points out that the three main cities contain thirty percent of the total population. This leaves the other two-thirds of the population dispersed throughout the nation, with quite a few cities having populations on the order or 25,000. Most of these cities are centers of agricultural communities.

The lecturer mentions that the industry of Kochen is centered in the capital city of Norkhan, but postpones a discussion of it. Norkhan is described as a pretty city. Many trees, flowers, and shrubs grow there because of the tropical climate. The Tarko River runs through the central plain where the rice is grown. The lecturer places Norkhan in the center of Kochen and points out that it is located on the banks of the Tarko River. The center for rice distribution is the capital city of Norkhan. The rice comes to Norkhan by barges which come down the Tarko River. There are rice storage warehouses in Norkhan. Kochen has no seaports, so the rice is shipped by rail through the countries which border Kochen to seaports for transshipment. He closes his lecture, saying that he will continue his discussion of Norkhan in the next lecture.

DICTATION

1. _____	1. _____
2. _____	2. _____
3. _____	3. _____
4. _____	4. _____
5. _____	5. _____
6. _____	6. _____
7. _____	7. _____
8. _____	8. _____
9. _____	9. _____
10. _____	10. _____
11. _____	11. _____
12. _____	12. _____
13. _____	13. _____
14. _____	14. _____
15. _____	15. _____
16. _____	16. _____
17. _____	17. _____
18. _____	18. _____
19. _____	19. _____
20. _____	20. _____
21. _____	21. _____

22. _____   22. _____

23. _____   23. _____

24. _____   24. _____

25. _____   25. _____

Number correct _____

AUDING PROMPT A

For the last couple of lectures, I've been talking about Kochen's agriculture. I'd like to leave this topic and discuss something else. If we have time later on, I may talk some more about agriculture. But now I'd like to talk about the population centers of Kochen.

Let's begin with the capital. The capital is Norkhan, which has a population of some 5,000,000 people. It is by far the largest city in the kingdom. The second largest metropolis is Norpin with about a million and a half. The other big city is Sumalark with about a million people. So you can see that in these three cities alone there is a population of roughly seven and a half million people. I forgot to mention that the total population of Kochen according to the 1975 census is 25,000,000 people. Thus, we thirty percent of the total populace concentrated in these three cities. The other two-thirds of the population is scattered throughout the kingdom, with many cities on the order of 25,000 people. These are primarily agricultural centers.

In Norkhan, the capital, we find concentrated what industry there is in the kingdom. I'll be explaining the nature of this a little later on. Norkhan itself is a rather pretty city. Given the kind of climate that there is in Kochen, trees, flowers, and shrubs grow in profusion. You will recall that the Tarko River runs through the central rice-growing plain. Norkhan is almost in the exact geographical center of the country and is located along the banks of the Tarko. Norkhan is the rice distribution center for the whole country. The rice, at least much of it, comes by river barges down the Tarko River to the city of Norkhan, where it is warehoused. Rice for export then moves by rail through neighboring countries which have seaports, Kochen being landlocked. I'll tell you a little more about Norkhan next time.

AUDING PROMPT B

_____ _____ last couple _____ lectures, _____ _____ talking about Kochen's agriculture. _____ _____ _____ leave this topic _____ discuss something else. _____ _____ _____ _____ later on, _____ may talk _____ more about agriculture. _____ now _____ like to talk about _____ population centers of Kochen.

_____ begin with _____ capital. _____ capital is Norkhan, _____ has a population of some 5,000,000 _____. _____ _____ by far _____ largest city in _____ kingdom. _____ second largest metropolis is Norpin with _____ _____ million and a half. _____ other big city is Sumalark with _____ _____ million people. _____ _____ _____ _____ _____ in these three cities _____ there is a population of roughly seven and a half million _____. _____ _____ _____ _____ _____ total population of Kochen according to _____ 1975 census is 25,000,000 _____ .Thus, _____ _____ thirty percent of _____ total populace concentrated in _____ three cities. _____ other two-thirds of _____ population _____ scattered throughout ____ kingdom, ____ many cities on ____ order of 25,000 ____. ____ ____ primarily agricultural centers.

In Norkhan, ____ ____, we find concentrated what industry there is ____ ____ ____. I'll be explaining ____ nature of this ____ ____ later on. Norkhan ____ ____ ____ rather pretty city. Given the ____ ____ climate ____ ____ ____ in Kochen, trees, flowers, and shrubs grow in profusion. ____ ____ recall ____ ____ Tarko River runs through ____ central rice-growing plain. Norkhan is almost in ____ exact geographical center of the country ____ ____ located along ____ banks of ____ Tarko. Norkhan is ____ rice distribution center for ____ whole country. ____ rice, ____ ____ much of it, comes by river barges down ____ Tarko ____ to ____ ____ ____ Norkhan, where ____ ____ warehoused. Rice for export ____ moves by rail through neighboring countries which have seaports, Kochen ____ landlocked. ____ ____ ____ ____ ____ more about Norkhan next time.

AUDING PROMPT C

—— last —— couple —— lectures —— Kochen's —— agriculture ——. —— leave —— topic ——. —— later —— may —— talk —— agriculture ——. —— now —— talk —— about —— population —— centers ——.

—— begin —— capital ——. —— capital —— Norkhan —— has —— population —— some —— 5,000,000 ——. —— by —— far —— largest —— city —— kingdom ——. —— second —— largest —— metropolis —— Norpin —— million —— and —— half ——. —— other —— big —— city —— Sumalark —— with —— million —— people ——. —— in —— three —— cities —— population —— roughly —— seven —— half —— million ——. —— total —— population —— Kochen —— 1975 —— census —— 25, 000,000 ——. —— thirty percent——total——populace——in——three cities ——. —— other —— two-thirds —— population —— scattered —— throughout —— kingdom —— many —— cities —— 25,000 ——. —— primarily —— agricultural —— centers ——.

—— in —— Norkhan —— find —— concentrated —— industry ——. —— explaining —— later ——. —— Norkhan —— pretty —— city ——. —— given —— climate —— trees —— flowers —— shrubs —— grow —— profusion ——. —— recall —— Tarko —— runs —— through —— central —— rice-growing —— plain ——. —— Norkhan —— almost —— exact —— geographical —— center —— country —— located —— banks —— Tarko ——. —— Norkhan —— rice —— distribution —— center —— whole —— country ——. —— rice —— comes —— by —— river —— barges —— down —— Tarko —— Norkhan -—— warehoused ——. —— rice —— export —— moves —— rail —— through —— neighboring —— countries —— have —— seaports —— Kochen —— landlocked ——. —— more —— Norkhan —— next —— time ——.

NOTES

Popln centers—Kochen

Capital—

    Norkhan—5,000,000, largest

    Norpin—1.5 million   7.5 mil.

    Sumalark—1 mil.

Total pop. = 25 mil. ('75 census)

30% of pop. in 3 cities

Many cities of 25,000—primarily agric. centers

Norkhan

    Industry conc. here

    Pretty city—trees, flowers, shrubs

Tarko R. runs thru centr. rice-growing plain

Nork. is in center of country, on banks of Tarko R.

    Rice distn. center

    Rice comes by barge down river to warehouses in Nork.

    Rice for export moves by rail thru neighboring countries w/ seaports;

    Kochen landlocked

YOUR NOTES

QUIZ

1. What is the capital city of Kochen?

2. Name the three largest cities in Kochen.

   _____

   _____

   _____

3. What percentage of the total population of Kochen lives in the three cities listed in 2, above?

4. In what city is Kochen's industry situated?

5. Locate the principal city of Kochen.

6. If Kochen is landlocked, how does rice get to seaports?

QUIZ ANSWERS

1. What is the capital city of Kochen?
   Norkhan

2. Name the three largest cities in Kochen.
   Norkhan
   Norpin
   Sumalark

3. What percentage of the total population of Kochen lives in the three cities listed in 2, above?
   30%

4. In what city is Kochen's industry situated?
   Norkhan

5. Locate the principal city of Kochen.
   On the banks of the Tarko River in the geographical center of the country.

6. If Kochen is landlocked, how does rice get to seaports?
   By rail through neighboring countries.

Norkhan

READING PREPARATION

The lecturer begins by reminding us that last time he mentioned that the population of Norkhan was 5,000,000 people. This made it the biggest city in the Kingdom of Kochen by far. He says that he now wants to discuss Norkhan's industry.

He says that rice exporting is the main industry. The warehouses which store the rice are situated on the outskirts of the city. The rice is stored here before being transshipped to other countries. The lecturer mentions two kinds of warehouses: government controlled and private-industry controlled. He says that the government warehouses store about a third of the rice. Actually, the government leases space to small exporters. The other two-thirds of the warehouses are in the hands of 15 different companies, all of which are in the business of exporting rice. He tells us that in some cases the companies grow their own rice, so that there is company control of the rice business from the time of growing until export.

He moves on to talk about small industry in Norkhan. First he describes the cotton fabric industry. Here, fabrics are printed with old Kochenese designs. He says that although the industry is rather small, it is nonetheless expanding. He notes that the Kochenese designs are becoming popular in the Western part of the world, and that demand for these cottons is growing. When the industry began only yard goods were produced, but there has been an expansion and small shops now produce tailored goods such as men's shirts, women's blouses, skirts, etc.

He tells of the famous Kochenese silver work; handwork done in small, one-man operations. He notes the growing tourist industry and its relationship with the cotton goods and silverware. He closes by telling of a new boat ride for tourists which is becoming popular, up the Tarko River.

DICTATION

1. _____	1. _____
2. _____	2. _____
3. _____	3. _____
4. _____	4. _____
5. _____	5. _____
6. _____	6. _____
7. _____	7. _____
8. _____	8. _____
9. _____	9. _____
10. _____	10. _____
11. _____	11. _____
12. _____	12. _____
13. _____	13. _____
14. _____	14. _____
15. _____	15. _____
16. _____	16. _____
17. _____	17. _____
18. _____	18. _____
19. _____	19. _____
20. _____	20. _____
21. _____	21. _____

22. _____   22. _____

23. _____   23. _____

24. _____   24. _____

25. _____   25. _____

Number correct ____

AUDING PROMPT A

Last time I told you that Norkhan has a population of 5,000,000 people which makes it by far the largest city in the kingdom of Kochen. Today I'd like to discuss with you the industry which goes on in Norkhan.

Of course the principal industry is that of rice exportation. On the outskirts of the city itself are located the warehouses which hold the rice prior to transshipment to other countries. The warehouses are of two types, those controlled by the government and those controlled by private industry. The government warehouses handle roughly one-third of the rice. Actually, what the government is involved in is the leasing of space to small exporters. The other two-thirds of the warehouses are owned by 15 separate companies which are in the rice exporting business. These companies, in some cases, grow their own rice, so that they control the rice business from the field right on through to the time it is exported.

There is some small industry in Norkhan as well. One of these is the printing of cotton fabrics with old Kochenese designs. While this is a comparatively small industry, nevertheless it is an expanding one. The Kochenese designs have caught on in the Western world and there is an increasing demand for Kochenese cottons. When the industry got started only yard goods were produced, but now there are some small shops which actually are producing tailored goods such as men's shirts, women's blouses, skirts, and so forth.

Let's see—what else is there? Well, the Kochenese have long been famous for their silver work. This is pretty much handwork and is done in very small, usually one-man operations. In addition to this, there is an ever-expanding tourist industry. Naturally, the two products I just mentioned, the cotton goods and the silver jewelry, appeal to the tourist trade. Recently two companies have begun boat rides up the Tarko River and this seems to be catching on. Time's up.

AUDING PROMPT B

_____ _____ _____ _____ _____ _____ Norkhan has _____ population of 5,000,000 _____ _____ _____ _____ by far _____ largest city in _____ _____ _____ Kochen. _____ _____ _____ _____ discuss _____ _____ _____ industry which goes on in Norkhan.

_____ _____ _____ principal industry is _____ _____ rice exportation. On _____ outskirts of _____ city _____ are located _____ warehouses which hold _____ rice prior to transshipment to other countries. _____ warehouses are _____ two types, _____ controlled by _____ government _____ _____ controlled by private industry. _____ government warehouses handle roughly one-third _____ _____ _____ . _____ , _____ _____ government is involved in _____ _____ leasing _____ space to small exporters. _____ other two-thirds of _____ warehouses _____ owned by 15 separate companies _____ _____ in _____ rice exporting business. _____ companies, in some cases, grow _____ own rice, so _____

_____ control _____ rice business from _____ field _____ _____ through _____ _____ time _____ _____ exported.

_____ _____ some small industry in Norkhan _____ _____. One _____ _____ is_____ printing of cotton fabrics with old Kochenese designs. While _____ _____ _____ comparatively small _____, nevertheless _____ _____ _____ expanding _____. _____ Kochenese designs have caught on in _____ Western world _____ _____ _____ an increasing demand for Kochenese cottons. When _____ industry _____ started only yard goods _____ produced, _____ now _____ _____ some small shops _____ _____ _____ producing tailored goods such as men's shirts, women's blouses, skirts, _____ _____ _____.

_____ _____—what else _____ _____? _____, _____ Kochenese _____ long been famous for _____ silver work. _____ _____ pretty much handwork _____ _____ done in very small, usually one-man operations. In addition _____ _____, _____ _____ an ever-expanding tourist industry. Naturally, _____ _____ _____ _____ _____ _____, _____ cotton goods and _____ silver jewelry, appeal to _____ tourist trade. Recently two companies have begun boat rides up _____ Tarko River _____ _____ seems to be catching on. _____ _____.

AUDING PROMPT C

—— Norkhan —— population —— 5,000,000 —— largest —— city —— Kochen ——. —— discuss —— industry —— Norkhan ——.

—— principal —— industry —— rice —— exportation ——. —— outskirts —— city —— located —— warehouses —— hold —— rice —— prior —— transshipment —— countries——. —— warehouses —— two —— types —— controlled —— government —— controlled —— private —— industry ——. —— government —— warehouses —— handle —— one-third ——. —— government —— involved —— leasing —— space —— small —— exporters ——. —— two-thirds —— warehouses —— owned —— 15 —— companies —— rice —— exporting ——. —— companies —— some —— cases —— grow —— own —— rice —— control —— rice —— business —— field —— through —— time —— exported ——.

—— some —— small —— industry —— Norkhan ——. —— one —— printing —— cotton —— fabrics —— old —— Kochenese —— designs ——. —— comparatively —— small —— expanding——. —— Kochenese —— designs —— caught on —— Western —— world —— increasing —— demand —— Kochenese —— cottons ——. —— industry —— started —— yard —— goods —— produced —— small —— shops —— producing —— tailored —— goods —— men's —— shirts —— women's —— blouses —— skirts ——.

—— Kochenese —— long —— famous —— silver —— work ——. —— handwork —— done —— small —— one-man —— operations——. —— ever-expanding —— tourist —— industry ——. —— cotton —— goods —— silver —— jewelry —— appeal —— tourist ——. —— two —— companies —— boat —— rides —— Tarko —— seems —— catching on ——.

NOTES

Industry—Norkhan

    Prin—rice exptn

        —warehouses on outskirts of city—hold rice prior to transshipment

            2 types—gov't cont.—handle 1/3

                —pvt. industry—handle 2/3

        —gov't leases space to sml. exporters

        —15 pvt. companies—some grow & ship rice

Small industry

    Cotton fabrics—old K designs

        Small but expanding

        Designs popular in West, demand increasing

        Yd. goods produced first, now shirts, blouses, skirts

    Silver work

        Handwork

        1-man operations

    Tourism

        Expanding

        Cotton/silver appeal to tourists

        2 co's have boat rides up Tarko, catching on

YOUR NOTES

QUIZ

1. What is the principal industry in Norkhan?

2. Where are the warehouses located which store the rice prior to shipment?
   ( ) In the heart of Norkhan
   ( ) Just outside Norkhan proper
   ( ) A considerable distance from Norkhan

3. Describe the kinds of warehouses Norkhan has and tell something about their function.

4. What small industries exist in Norkhan?

QUIZ ANSWERS

1. What is the principal industry in Norkhan?
   Rice exportation. (or) Exporting rice.

2. Where are the warehouses located which store the rice prior to shipment?
   ( ) In the heart of Norkhan
   (X) Just outside Norkhan proper
   ( ) A considerable distance from Norkhan

3. Describe the kinds of warehouses Norkhan has and tell something about their function.
   Two types: gov't controlled and private industry controlled. Gov't warehouses are leased to small exporters. Gov't warehouses control 1/3 of the rice; private industry, 2/3.

4. What small industries exist in Norkhan?
   Cotton fabrics with Kochenese designs
   Silver jewelry
   Tourism

The Monarchy

READING PREPARATION

The lecturer begins by giving a last note on light industry in Norkhan. He mentions that there is a variety of handicrafts such as wood carving, lacquerware, and the weaving of table mats. He notes that they are all small, cottage-industry kinds of operations involving a family or an extended family. He says that there isn't any heavy industry because Kochen lacks mineral deposits of any consequence. He adds, parenthetically, that Norkhan isn't plagued by smog. He suggests that if you want to read about the small industries, the subject is covered in a recent publication by Arthur Smedley entitled *Kochenese Handicrafts* or *The Handicrafts of Kochen* or some similar title. He points out that the book is in the library and the author is a long-time resident of Kochen.

The lecturer then turns to the political structure of Kochen and takes a look at how it is governed at the national and local levels. He says that Kochen is classified as a constitutional monarchy, but that in actuality it is an absolute monarchy, and says he will explain why this is so. Queen Pingpum Sowatsam, 77, is the ruling monarch. The prime minister is her son and is heir to the throne; thus, in a sense, Kochen is an absolute monarchy because "it's all in the family." The name of the prime minister is Det Sowatsam. The lecturer says that he is a very able man and under his guidance the country has enjoyed political calm for the last two decades. The queen has another son, Nek Sowatsam, also an able politician. He is the minister of foreign affairs. The queen is in the driver's seat, and with her two sons in two of the top ministerial posts, the government is safely in the Sowatsam family's hands.

When Det and Nek were in their infancy, the lecturer notes, the king died of cholera. Now the brothers are 50 and 47, very close, and completely devoted to their mother. He closes by saying that he'll be talking some more about the government at the next meeting.

DICTATION

1. _____   1. _____

2. _____   2. _____

3. _____   3. _____

4. _____   4. _____

5. _____   5. _____

6. _____   6. _____

7. _____   7. _____

8. _____   8. _____

9. _____   9. _____

10. _____   10. _____

11. _____   11. _____

12. _____   12. _____

13. _____   13. _____

14. _____   14. _____

15. _____   15. _____

16. _____   16. _____

17. _____   17. _____

18. _____   18. _____

19. _____   19. _____

20. _____   20. _____

21. _____   21. _____

22. _____   22. _____

23. _____   23. _____

24. _____   24. _____

25. _____   25. _____

Number correct _____

AUDING PROMPT A

One final note about light industry in Norkhan. There are a variety of handicrafts such as wood carving, lacquerware, and weaving of such things as table mats. All of these are small, often cottage-industry types of operations involving a family or an extended family. Kochen lacks mineral deposits of any consequence, so that there is no heavy industry. Parenthetically, I might add that Norkhan is not plagued by smog, either. If you're interested in reading up on the small industries in Kochen, the subject is covered rather well in a recent book by Arthur Smedley. It's called *Kochenese Handicrafts* or *The Handicrafts of Kochen,* something like that. Anyway, it's over in the library and the author is a long-time resident of Kochen.

I'd like to turn now to the political structure of Kochen and take a look at how it is governed at the national level and at the local level. Let's begin at the top and work down. Kochen is classified as a constitutional monarchy, but in actuality it is almost an absolute monarchy. I'll explain why I say this in a minute. The ruling monarch is Queen Pingpum Sowatsam, who is now 77 years old. Her son, the heir to the throne, is the prime minister and this is why I say that for all practical purposes, Kochen is an absolute monarchy. It's sort of all in the family, so to speak. The prime minister, whose name is Det Sowatsam, is a very able man and the country has enjoyed political calm over the past couple of decades. The queen's other son, Nek Sowatsam, is also a very able politician. He is the minister of foreign affairs. So you see, with the mother in the driver's seat, and her two sons in the two top ministerial posts, the government is safely in the hands of the Sowatsam family.

The king died many years ago of cholera when his sons, Det and Nek, were in their infancy. The brothers, 50 and 47, are very close and entirely devoted to their mother, the queen. I'll be talking more about the government next meeting.

AUDING PROMPT B

_____ final note about light industry in Norkhan. _____ _____ _____ variety of handicrafts such as wood carving, lacquerware, and weaving _____ such things as table mats. All _____ _____ are small, often cottage-industry _____ _____ operations involving _____ family or _____ extended family. Kochen lacks mineral deposits of any consequence, so _____ _____ _____ no heavy industry. _____, _____ _____ _____ _____ Norkhan _____ not plagued by smog, _____. If you're interested in reading up on _____ small industries in Kochen, _____ subject _____ covered _____ well in _____ recent book by Arthur Smedley. _____ called *Kochenese Handicrafts* or *The Handicrafts of Kochen,* something like that. _____, _____ _____ in _____ library _____ _____ author is _____ long-time resident of Kochen.

_____ _____ _____ turn now to _____ political structure of Kochen _____

_____ _____ look at how _____ _____ governed at _____ national level and _____ _____ local level. _____ begin at _____ top and work down. Kochen _____ classified as _____ constitutional monarchy, but in actuality _____ is almost _____ absolute monarchy. I'll explain why _____ _____ _____ _____ _____ _____. _____ ruling monarch is Queen Pingpum Sowatsam, _____ _____ _____ 77 _____ _____. Her son, _____ heir to _____ throne, is _____ prime minister _____ this is why _____ _____ _____ for all practical purposes, Kochen is _____ absolute monarchy. _____ _____ _____ _____ in the family, _____ _____ _____. _____ prime minister, _____ name _____ Det Sowatsam, _____ _____ very able _____ _____ _____ country has enjoyed political calm over _____ past couple _____ decades. _____ queen's other son, Nek Sowatsam, _____ also _____ very able politician. He is _____ minister of foreign affairs. _____ _____ _____, with _____ mother in _____ driver's seat, _____ _____ two sons in _____ two top ministerial posts, _____ government _____ safely in _____ hands of _____ Sowatsam family.

_____ king died many years ago of cholera when _____ sons, Det and Nek, were in _____ infancy. _____ brothers, 50 and 47, are very close _____ entirely devoted to their mother, _____ _____. _____ _____ talking more about _____ government next meeting.

AUDING PROMPT C

—— final —— note —— light —— industry —— Norkhan ——. —— variety —— handicrafts —— wood carving —— lacquerware —— weaving —— table mats ——. —— all —— small —— cottage-industry —— operations —— involving —— family —— extended —— family ——. —— Kochen —— lacks —— mineral —— deposits —— any —— consequence —— no —— heavy —— industry ——. —— Norkhan —— not —— plagued —— smog ——. —— if —— interested —— reading up —— small —— industries —— Kochen —— subject —— covered —— well —— in —— book —— Arthur —— Smedley ——. —— called —— *Kochenese* —— *Handicrafts* —— or ——*Handicrafts* —— of —— *Kochen* ——. —— in —— library —— author —— resident —— Kochen ——.

—— turn —— to —— political —— structure —— Kochen —— how —— governed —— national —— level —— local —— level ——. —— Kochen —— classified —— constitutional —— monarchy —— in —— actuality —— absolute —— monarchy ——. —— monarch —— Queen Pingpum Sowatsam —— 77 ——. —— son —— heir —— prime —— minister —— for —— practical —— purposes —— Kochen —— absolute —— monarchy ——. —— prime —— minister —— Det Sowatsam —— able —— country —— enjoyed —— political —— calm —— over —— past —— couple —— decades ——. —— queen's —— other —— son —— Nek Sowatsam —— also —— able —— politician —— minister —— of —— foreign —— affairs ——. ——

mother —— driver's —— seat —— two —— sons —— top —— ministerial —— posts —— government —— in —— hands —— Sowatsam —— family ——.

—— king —— died —— years —— ago —— cholera —— sons —— Det —— Nek —— in —— infancy ——. —— brothers —— 50 —— 47 —— very —— close —— devoted —— to —— mother ——. —— more —— about —— government —— next ——.

NOTES

Light industry (Norkhan)

> Variety of handicrafts—wood carving, lacquerware, weaving (table mats)

> Small, cottage-industry; family/extended fam.

No mineral deposits = no heavy industry = no smog!

Ref. Smedley, Arthur, *Koch. Handicrafts* or *The Handicrafts of Koch.* in lib.

Political struc.

> Const. monarchy—but actually absolute (???)

> Monarch—Queen Pingpum Sowatsam, 77

> Son—heir to throne, is P.M.

>> Det Sowatsam—able ∴ country has had political calm for 2 decades

>> Nek S., other son, is min. of for. affairs, also able

> Mom—Queen; 2 sons top ministers = family control of gov't

> King—died of cholera when Det & Nek were babies; bros. are close, de-

>> voted to Queen

YOUR NOTES

QUIZ

1. Why does Kochen not have heavy industry?

2. What form of government does Kochen have?
   ( ) Monarchy
   ( ) Absolute monarchy
   ( ) Constitutional monarchy
   ( ) All of the above

3. What is the name of Kochen's monarch?

4. Technically speaking, Kochen's government fits one of the categories in Question 2. What did the lecturer say is the practical or real situation which obtains in Kochen re the government and what were his reasons for making the statement?

5. What was the fate of the king of Kochen?

QUIZ ANSWERS

1. Why does Kochen not have heavy industry?
   No mineral deposits of any consequence.

2. What form of government does Kochen have?
   ( ) Monarchy
   ( ) Absolute monarchy
   (X) Constitutional monarchy
   ( ) All of the above

3. What is the name of Kochen's monarch?
   Pingpum Sowatsam

4. Technically speaking, Kochen's government fits one of the categories in Question 2. What did the lecturer say is the practical or real situation which obtains in Kochen re the government and what were his reasons for making the statement?
   Kochen is an "absolute" monarchy because the Queen's two sons hold the posts of prime minister and minister of foreign affairs. Thus, the Sowatsam family controls the government.

5. What was the fate of the king of Kochen?
   Died of cholera many years ago.

Queen Pingpum Sowatsam

READING PREPARATION

The subject of this lecture is the queen of Kochen, Pingpum Sowatsam, who is "quite a gal," according to the lecturer. He claims that at age 77, she has more energy and drive than most teen-agers. He says that she lets her son, Det, who is the prime minister, rule the country, but that there is little question that the real power is held by her. He goes on to say that the queen doesn't abuse her power.

Queen Pingpum is described as rather tall for a Kochenese woman, in that she stands 5'8". And, as he pointed out before, she is a very active person. She not only participates in a multitude of government activities and ceremonies, but is also active in athletics. Several times a week she plays badminton, and if her busy schedule will permit it, she plays it daily. The lecturer continues that she also likes to swim and does so almost every morning in the pool which is on the grounds of the palace. When she was young, he says, she was an ardent tennis player and represented Kochen once at Wimbledon in England. At age 65 she gave up tennis for the somewhat less strenuous sport of badminton.

The lecturer says that the queen received her education in Kochen and abroad. She went through high school in Kochen, and then did her university studies in England. Her bachelor's degree is in political science, which was very unusual for any woman at the time she did it. She had a nearly perfect record and was an honor student. He goes on to say that after she finished her education in England, she came back to Kochen. Shortly after her return she married Kochen's crown prince, who ascended to the throne after his father died. Unfortunately, it was a short marriage because the king contracted cholera while on a trip to one of the most distant parts of the kingdom. By the time it was possible to get medical assistance, the king had died. In those days, the lecturer reminds us, there were no helicopters. The queen took her new duties in stride and has reigned since then. Without doubt she is one of the most remarkable women in Southeast Asia.

DICTATION

1. _____   1. _____

2. _____   2. _____

3. _____   3. _____

4. _____   4. _____

5. _____   5. _____

6. _____   6. _____

7. _____   7. _____

8. _____   8. _____

9. _____   9. _____

10. _____   10. _____

11. _____   11. _____

12. _____   12. _____

13. _____   13. _____

14. _____   14. _____

15. _____   15. _____

16. _____   16. _____

17. _____   17. _____

18. _____   18. _____

19. _____   19. _____

20. _____   20. _____

21. _____   21. _____

22. _____   22. _____

23. _____   23. _____

24. _____   24. _____

25. _____   25. _____

Number correct _____

AUDING PROMPT A

The queen of Kochen, Pingpum Sowatsam, is, to put it mildly, quite a gal! At age 77, she can put most teen-agers to shame when it comes to energy and drive. Although she lets her son, Det, rule the country in his capacity as prime minister, there is no question that she holds the real power. However, I must admit that she doesn't abuse her power.

Queen Pingpum is rather tall for a Kochenese woman, standing 5'8". As I've already indicated she is a very active person. Not only does she participate in a multitude of government activities and other ceremonies, but she also takes an active interest in athletics. She plays badminton several times a week and daily if her busy schedule will allow it. She also likes to swim and it is reported that she swims almost every morning in the pool on the palace grounds. In her younger days, she was an ardent tennis player and once represented Kochen at Wimbledon in England. She gave up tennis at age 65 for the slightly less strenuous sport of badminton.

The queen was educated both in her own country and abroad. She attended schools in Kochen through high school and then went to England for her university training. She took a bachelor's degree in political science, which was most unusual for any woman at that time. She was an honor student with a nearly perfect record. Following her education in England, she returned to Kochen. Shortly after her return she married the crown prince of Kochen, who ascended the throne upon the death of his father. Unfortunately, the marriage was not to last too long because the king was taken sick with cholera on a trip to one of the most remote parts of the kingdom. By the time medical assistance was available—remember in those days there weren't any helicopters—it was too late and the king had died. Queen Pingpum took her new duties in stride and has reigned ever since. She is truly one of the most remarkable women in all of Southeast Asia.

AUDING PROMPT B

_____ queen of Kochen, Pingpum Sowatsam, is, _____ _____ _____ _____, quite a gal! At age 77, _____ _____ put most teen-agers to shame when _____ comes to energy and drive. Although _____ lets her son, Det, rule _____ country _____ _____ _____ as prime minister, _____ _____ no question _____ she holds the real power. However, _____ _____ _____ _____ she doesn't abuse her power.

_____ Pingpum _____ rather tall for _____ Kochenese woman, _____ 5'8". _____ _____ _____ _____ _____ _____ _____ very active person. _____ _____ she participate in _____ multitude of government activities _____ other ceremonies, _____ _____ also takes _____ active interest in athletics. _____ plays badminton several times a week _____ daily if _____ busy schedule will allow _____. _____ _____ likes to swim _____ _____ _____ reported _____ she swims almost every morning _____ _____ _____ _____ _____ _____ _____. In

_____ younger days, _____ was _____ ardent tennis player _____ once represented Kochen at Wimbledon _____ England. _____ gave up tennis at age 65 for _____ _____ less strenuous sport _____ badminton.

_____ queen was educated _____ in _____ own country and abroad. _____ attended schools in Kochen through high school _____ then went to England for _____ university _____. _____ took _____ bachelor's degree in political science, _____ _____ most unusual for any woman at that time. _____ was _____ honor student with _____ nearly perfect record. Following _____ education in England, _____ returned to Kochen. Shortly after _____ return _____ married _____ crown prince of Kochen, who ascended _____ throne upon _____ death of his father. Unfortunately, _____ marriage was not to last too long because _____ king _____ taken sick with cholera on _____ trip to _____ _____ _____ most remote parts of the kingdom. By the time medical assistance _____ available— _____ in those days _____ weren't any helicopters—_____ _____ too late and _____ king had died. _____ Pingpum took _____ new duties in stride _____ has reigned ever since. _____ _____ truly one of _____ most remarkable women in _____ _____ Southeast Asia.

AUDING PROMPT C

—— queen —— Kochen —— Pingpum Sowatsam —— quite —— gal ——. —— age —— 77 —— put —— most —— teen-agers —— shame —— comes —— energy —— drive ——. —— although —— lets —— son —— Det —— rule —— country —— prime —— minister —— no —— question —— she —— holds —— real —— power ——. —— doesn't —— abuse —— power ——.

—— Pingpum —— rather —— tall —— Kochenese —— woman —— 5'8" ——. —— very —— active —— person ——. —— participate —— multitude —— government —— activities —— ceremonies —— also —— takes —— interest —— athletics ——. —— plays —— badminton —— several —— times —— week —— daily —— if —— busy —— schedule —— allow ——. —— likes —— swim —— reported —— swims —— almost —— every —— morning ——. —— younger —— days —— ardent —— tennis —— player —— represented —— Kochen —— Wimbledon —— England ——. —— gave —— up —— tennis —— 65 —— less —— strenuous —— sport —— badminton ——.

—— queen —— educated —— own —— country —— abroad ——. —— attended —— schools —— Kochen —— through —— high school —— England —— university ——. —— took —— bachelor's —— political —— science —— most —— unusual —— for —— woman —— that —— time ——. —— honor —— student —— nearly —— perfect —— record——. —— following —— England —— returned —— Kochen. Shortly —— after —— returned —— married —— crown —— prince —— Kochen —— who —— ascended —— throne —— upon —— death —— father ——. —— marriage —— not —— last —— long —— king —— taken —— sick —— cholera —— trip —— remote —— parts —— kingdom ——. —— by —— time —— medical —— assistance —— available —— those —— days —— weren't —— helicopters —— too —— late —— king —— died ——. —— Pingpum —— took —— duties —— stride —— reigned —— since ——. —— truly —— remarkable —— women —— Southeast —— Asia ——.

NOTES

Queen Pingpum Sowatsam—"swinger"

77, energetic, driver

Son Det rules as P.M., but P.S. holds real power—doesn't abuse power

Tall for Kochenese—5'8"

Athletic

Plays badminton several times/wk, daily if possible

Swims almost daily

Played tennis when young, rep. Kochen at Wimbledon, Eng.

Gave up tennis at 65 for badminton

Educ^n

H.S. in Kochen

Eng. for B.A., Pol Sci—honor student, nearly perfect record

Returned to Kochen after educ^n, married crown prince—became king

after father's death

Marriage didn't last—king died of cholera on trip to remote area

P.S. took over & has reigned since

One of most remarkable ♀ in S.E.A.

YOUR NOTES

QUIZ

1. Describe briefly Queen Pingpum Sowatsam's athletic interests.

2. Where did the queen of Kochen receive her education?

3. What was the extent of Queen Pingpum's formal education?

4. How was Queen Pingpum rated as a student?

5. Whom did Queen Pingpum marry?

6. Describe the circumstances under which Queen Pingpum became Kochen's monarch.

QUIZ ANSWERS

1. Describe briefly Queen Pingpum Sowatsam's athletic interests.
   Swims daily, plays badminton as often as she can, played tennis when younger—once represented Kochen at Wimbledon.

2. Where did the queen of Kochen receive her education?
   In Kochen (high school) and England (university).

3. What was the extent of Queen Pingpum's formal education?
   B.A. in Political Science (England).

4. How was Queen Pingpum rated as a student?
   Excellent (or) Honors (or) First rate

5. Whom did Queen Pingpum marry?
   The crown prince of Kochen.

6. Describe the circumstances under which Queen Pingpum became Kochen's monarch.
   Her husband, the king, died of cholera while on a trip to a remote area of Kochen.

Transportation

READING PREPARATION

The topic of this lecture is transportation in Kochen, and the lecturer points out that there are three main types: water, air, and land. He says that many small rivers traverse the kingdom, so small-boat transportation is very common. Many goods, therefore, come to market by means of water transportation.

The next point is that there is a state-owned and -operated railway system. This system, which was built by a German contracting firm in 1916, has served Kochen's needs quite well even though some of the equipment is a little outdated. The lecturer claims that there is a rustic charm to the old-fashioned coaches which are still used. Although a fair number of people use this transportation method, its main use is for the movement of goods, primarily rice, to Norkhan, the capital.

He mentions that in addition to the railroads, there is a bus system operating on a rather sporadic timetable. The bodies of the buses are made in Norkhan, but the chassis are imported. These buses are said to be the most colorful in the world. Several small companies operate the buses and compete with each other in decorating their buses. He says that one sees buses with handsomely carved bodies painted a variety of colors. The buses are open-air, which is quite suitable given the climatic conditions in Kochen.

A fair number of privately-owned taxis are found in the capital city. A person must bargain for his fare because there are no meters. This is no problem to the Kochenese, of course, but it sometimes poses a bit of a headache to the tourists. Because so few of the taxi drivers speak English, some rather comical situations arise. The lecturer adds that it is fortunate that the Kochenese are a very kind and easy-going people, so usually nobody gets very angry.

In 1968, he says, the Kochenese government began to operate a small airline which flies between cities in Kochen and to adjacent countries as well. The Kochenese have not yet started an overseas airline for prestige purposes. Service, he says, is good on Air Kochen.

DICTATION

1. _____   1. _____

2. _____   2. _____

3. _____   3. _____

4. _____   4. _____

5. _____   5. _____

6. _____   6. _____

7. _____   7. _____

8. _____   8. _____

9. _____   9. _____

10. _____   10. _____

11. _____   11. _____

12. _____   12. _____

13. _____   13. _____

14. _____   14. _____

15. _____   15. _____

16. _____   16. _____

17. _____   17. _____

18. _____   18. _____

19. _____   19. _____

20. _____   20. _____

21. _____   21. _____

22. _____   22. _____

23. _____   23. _____

24. _____   24. _____

25. _____   25. _____

Number correct _____

AUDING PROMPT A

Transportation in Kochen is, as elsewhere, of three main types: water, air, and land. There are many small rivers which traverse the kingdom, so transportation by small boats is quite common. A lot of goods come to market by means of water transportation.

There is a state-owned and -operated railway system. This system was built by a German contracting firm in 1916 and although some of the equipment is a little outdated, it serves Kochen's needs quite well. There is a certain rustic charm to the old-fashioned coaches which are still in use. A fair number of people use this method of transportation, but its main use is, of course, for the movement of goods, in the main rice, to the capital city of Norkhan.

In addition to the railway system mentioned, there is also a bus system which operates on a rather sporadic timetable. The chassis of the bus is imported and then the body is made in Norkhan. These buses are perhaps the most colorful in the world. There are several small companies operating these bus lines and they seem to try to outdo each other in decorating their buses. So, you see buses with rather handsomely carved bodies painted a variety of colors. These are open-air buses which are really rather suitable given the climatic conditions which obtain in Kochen.

In the capital city, one finds a fair number of privately-owned taxis. There are no meters, so one has to bargain for his fare. To the Kochenese, this is no problem, but to the tourists this sometimes poses a bit of a headache. Very few of the taxi drivers speak any English, so some rather comical situations arise. Fortunately, the Kochenese are a very kind and easy-going people, so usually nobody gets very angry.

In 1968, the Kochenese government began to operate a small airline which flies between cities in Kochen and also to adjacent countries. However, the Kochenese have not yet started an overseas airline for prestige purposes. Service is good on Air Kochen.

AUDING PROMPT B

Transportation in Kochen is, _____ _____, _____ three main types: water, air, _____ land. _____ _____ many small rivers _____ traverse _____ kingdom, _____ transportation by small boats _____ quite common. A lot of goods come to market by _____ _____ water transportation.

_____ _____ _____ state-owned and -operated railway system. _____ system _____ built by _____ German contracting firm in 1916 _____ although some _____ _____ equipment _____ _____ little outdated, _____ serves Kochen's needs _____ well. _____ _____ _____ certain rustic charm to _____ old-fashioned coaches _____ _____ still in use. _____ fair number of people use this

_____ _____ transportation, but _____ main use _____, _____ _____, for _____ movement of goods, in the main rice, to _____ _____ _____ _____ Norkhan.

In addition to _____ railway _____ _____ _____, _____ _____ also _____ bus system which operates on _____ rather sporadic timetable. _____ chassis of _____ bus _____ imported _____ _____ _____ body _____ made in Norkhan. _____ buses _____ perhaps _____ most colorful in _____ world. _____ _____ several small companies operating _____ bus lines _____ _____ seem to try to outdo each other in decorating _____ buses. _____, you see buses with _____ handsomely carved bodies painted _____ variety of colors. _____ _____ open-air buses _____ _____ _____ rather suitable given _____ climatic conditions _____ _____ in Kochen.

In _____ capital city, one finds _____ fair number _____ privately-owned taxis. _____ _____ no meters, _____ one has to bargain for _____ fare. To _____ Kochenese, _____ _____ no problem, but to _____ tourists _____ sometimes poses _____ _____ _____ a headache. Very few _____ _____ taxi drivers speak _____ English, so some rather comical situations arise. Fortunately, _____ Kochenese _____ _____ very kind _____ easy-going people, _____ usually nobody gets very angry.

In 1968, _____ Kochenese government began _____ operate _____ small airline _____ flies between cities in Kochen and _____ to adjacent countries. _____, _____ Kochenese have not yet started _____ overseas airline for prestige _____. Service _____ good on Air Kochen.

AUDING PROMPT C

—— transportation —— Kochen —— three —— types —— water —— air —— land ——. —— many —— small —— rivers —— traverse —— kingdom —— transportation —— small —— boats —— common ——. —— goods —— come —— market —— water —— transportation ——.

—— state-owned —— -operated —— railway ——. —— built —— German —— contracting —— firm —— 1916 —— some —— equipment —— outdated —— serves —— needs —— well ——. —— rustic —— charm —— old-fashioned —— coaches ——. —— fair —— number —— people —— use —— method —— transportation —— main —— use —— movement —— goods —— rice —— to —— Norkhan ——.

—— bus —— system —— operates —— sporadic —— timetable ——. —— chassis —— bus —— imported —— body —— made —— Norkhan ——. —— buses —— most —— colorful —— world ——. —— several —— small —— companies —— operating —— bus lines —— try —— outdo —— each —— other —— decorating ——. —— buses. —— handsomely —— carved —— bodies —— painted —— variety —— colors ——. —— open-air —— buses —— suitable —— given —— climatic —— conditions ——.

—— capital —— fair —— number —— privately-owned —— taxis ——

—— no —— meters —— bargain —— for —— fare ——. —— Kochenese
—— no —— problem —— tourists —— poses —— headache ——. —— few
—— taxi —— drivers —— speak —— English —— some —— comical ——
situations ——. —— fortunately —— Kochenese —— very —— kind ——
easy-going —— usually —— nobody —— angry ——.

—— 1968 —— Kochenese —— government —— began —— operate ——
small —— airline —— flies —— between —— cities —— Kochen —— and
—— adjacent —— countries ——. —— Kochenese —— not —— yet ——
started —— overseas —— airline —— prestige ——. —— service —— good
—— Air Kochen ——.

NOTES

Transport[n]

>   Water—air—land

>   Many small rivers, small-boat transp. common

>   Goods move to mkt. by H_2O

Railway

>   St. owned/operated

>   Built by Germans—1916

>   Somewhat outdated, still functional

>   Main use—rice to Norkhan

>   Other II —people

Bus

>   Sporadic timetable

>   Chassis imported, body made in Norkhan

>   Colorful—beautifully carved

>   Open-air, fits climate

Taxis

>   In Norkhan

>   Privately-owned

>   No meters, bargaining = headache for tourists, drivers don't speak Eng.

>>   More nuisance than real problem

Airline (Air Kochen)

  Begun 1968 by K. gov't

  Intra-country, also to adjacent countries

  No overseas airline

  Service good

YOUR NOTES

QUIZ

1. What are the principal means by which goods are transported in Kochen?

2. Who owns the railway system in Kochen?

3. How would you characterize the railway system of Kochen?

4. What is unique about Kochen's bus system?

5. Why do tourists experience some difficulty with taxis in Norkhan?

6. What is the name of the domestic airline in Kochen and when did it begin its operations?

QUIZ ANSWERS

1. What are the principal means by which goods are transported in Kochen?
   Water, rail

2. Who owns the railway system in Kochen?
   The government (or) The state

3. How would you characterize the railway system of Kochen?
   A little outdated, but serviceable (or) Old-fashioned, but adequate

4. What is unique about Kochen's bus system?
   The bodies of the buses are highly decorated (or) Highly decorative bus bodies

5. Why do tourists experience some difficulty with taxis in Norkhan?
   No meters in the taxis and the drivers don't speak English.

6. What is the name of the domestic airline in Kochen and when did it begin its operations?
   Air Kochen—1968

Population

READING PREPARATION

The lecturer begins by saying that in an earlier lecture he mentioned that the population of Kochen is 25,000,000 according to the 1975 census. He adds that he'd mentioned that the capital, Norkhan, had 5,000,000 and was the largest city. Norpin, with a population of 1,500,000, is next in size, and Sumalark is the next with approximately a million people.

He then points out that the country has three centers of population. In addition, there are many small towns scattered throughout the country. Many of these, he says, are hamlets with five to ten thousand people. A typical hamlet consists of a Buddhist temple at the center, a small group of various kinds of shops, and a government office building for whatever government officials are appropriate. He notes that the villagers themselves live varying distances from the center of the village. No residential district as such exists. A bus line serves most of these villages, so they are eventually connected to one of the principal cities.

He poses the question, Who are the Kochenese? He answers that this is not an easy question. The Kochenese resemble the Thais, the Burmese, and the Vietnamese. According to one theory, the Kochenese are a mixture of southern peoples, those from Indonesia and Malaysia, and those from the north, the Chinese. If this theory is true, he says, the mixing happened a long time ago. Undoubtedly, he says, indigenous tribes lived in the area and intermarried with these people. He continues that the modern-day Kochenese have been in the area for a long time and have acquired their own characteristics. The Kochenese are, on the average, a little taller than their neighbors, the Thais, and there is no established reason for this. Diet has been suggested as a factor, but this is speculation.

Today's ethnic mix is about 90 percent Kochenese, 5 percent Chinese, and 5 percent others such as Europeans, Americans, etc.

DICTATION

1. _____	1. _____
2. _____	2. _____
3. _____	3. _____
4. _____	4. _____
5. _____	5. _____
6. _____	6. _____
7. _____	7. _____
8. _____	8. _____
9. _____	9. _____
10. _____	10. _____
11. _____	11. _____
12. _____	12. _____
13. _____	13. _____
14. _____	14. _____
15. _____	15. _____
16. _____	16. _____
17. _____	17. _____
18. _____	18. _____
19. _____	19. _____
20. _____	20. _____
21. _____	21. _____

22. _____   22. _____

23. _____   23. _____

24. _____   24. _____

25. _____   25. _____

Number correct _____

AUDING PROMPT A

In an earlier lecture I told you that the population of Kochen, according to the 1975 census, is 25,000,000. I think I also mentioned that the capital city of Norkhan has some 5,000,000 and is by far the largest city. Next in size is the city of Norpin with its population of a million and a half, and the next city of any size is Sumalark with roughly a million people.

So you see we have three population centers in the country. There are, of course, many many small towns scattered throughout the kingdom. Many of these are hamlets of five to ten thousand people. A typical hamlet would have a Buddhist temple at the center, a small group of shops of various kinds, and a government office building which would house whatever government officials were appropriate for the hamlet. The villagers would live varying distances from the village center, but there would be no residential district as such. Most of these farm villages are served by a bus line which eventually connects to one of the principal cities.

Who are the Kochenese? Well, that is not an easy question to answer. Physically, the Kochenese resemble the Thais, the Burmese, the Vietnamese, and so forth. One theory is that the Kochenese are a mixture of peoples who came from the south, that is, the peoples from Indonesia and Malaysia, and the people from the north, the Chinese. Of course, if this is true, it all happened a long time ago. Undoubtedly, there were indigenous tribes living in the area and quite naturally there would be some intermarriage with these people. The present-day Kochenese have been in the area a long time and have developed their own characteristics. On the average, the Kochenese are a little taller than their neighbors, the Thais, and one wonders why this is so. Some have suggested diet as a factor, but again this is speculation.

The present ethnic mix is about 90 percent Kochenese, with some 5 percent Chinese and 5 percent others including Europeans, Americans, and what have you.

AUDING PROMPT B

____ ____ earlier lecture ____ told you ____ ____ population of Kochen, according to ____ 1975 census, ____ 25,000,000. ____ ____ ____ also mentioned ____ ____ capital city ____ ____ has ____ 5,000,000 ____ is by far ____ largest ____. Next in size ____ ____ ____ ____ Norpin with ____ population of ____ million and ____ half, ____ ____ next city ____ ____ ____ is Sumalark ____ roughly a million ____.

____ ____ ____ ____ ____ three population centers in ____ country. There are, ____ ____, ____ many small towns scattered throughout ____ kingdom. Many ____ ____ are hamlets ____ five to ten thousand ____. ____ typical hamlet would have ____ Buddhist temple at ____ center, ____

small group of shops of various kinds, ____ ____ government office building ____ would house ____ government officials ____ appropriate for ____ hamlet. ____ villagers ____ live varying distances from ____ ____ center, but ____ ____ ____ no residential district ____ ____. Most ____ ____ farm villages ____ served by ____ bus ____ which eventually connects to one of ____ principal cities.

Who are ____ Kochenese? ____, ____ ____ not ____ easy question to answer. Physically, ____ Kochenese resemble ____ Thais, ____ Burmese, ____ Vietnamese, ____ ____ ____. One theory is that ____ Kochenese are ____ mixture of peoples ____ ____ from ____ south, ____ ____, ____ peoples from Indonesia and Malaysia, and ____ people from ____ north, ____ Chinese. ____ ____, if ____ ____ true, ____ all happened ____ long time ago. Undoubtedly, ____ ____ indigenous tribes living in ____ area ____ ____ naturally ____ ____ be ____ intermarriage ____. ____ ____. ____ present-day Kochenese have been in ____ area ____ long time ____ have developed ____ own characteristics. On the average, ____ Kochenese ____ ____ little taller than ____ ____, ____ Thais, ____ one wonders why ____ ____ ____. Some have suggested diet as ____ factor, ____ ____ this is speculation.

____ present ethnic mix ____ about 90 percent Kochenese, ____ ____ 5 percent Chinese ____ 5 percent others including Europeans, Americans, ____ ____ ____ ____.

AUDING PROMPT C

—— earlier —— lecture —— told —— population —— Kochen —— 1975 —— census —— 25,000,000 ——. —— mentioned —— capital —— has —— 5,000,000 —— largest —— city ——. —— next —— Norpin —— population —— million —— and —— half —— next —— city —— Sumalark —— roughly —— million ——.

—— three —— population —— centers ——. —— many —— small —— towns —— scattered —— throughout —— kingdom ——. —— many —— hamlets —— five —— ten —— thousand ——. —— typical —— hamlet —— Buddhist —— temple —— center —— small —— group —— shops —— various —— kinds —— government —— office —— building —— house —— government —— officials —— appropriate —— hamlet ——. —— villagers —— live —— varying —— distances —— from —— center —— no —— residential —— district ——. —— most —— villages —— served —— by —— bus —— eventually —— connects —— one —— principal —— cities ——.

—— who —— are —— Kochenese ——? —— not —— easy —— question ——. —— Kochenese —— resemble —— Thais —— Burmese —— Vietnamese ——. —— one —— theory —— is —— Kochense —— mixture

—— people —— from —— south —— Indonesia —— Malaysia —— and —— people —— from —— north —— Chinese ——. —— if —— true —— happened —— long —— time —— ago ——. —— undoubtedly —— indigenous —— tribes —— living —— area —— intermarriage ——. —— present-day —— Kochenese —— been —— in —— area —— long —— time —— developed —— own —— characteristics ——. —— Kochenese —— little —— taller —— than —— Thais —— one —— wonders —— why ——. —— some —— suggested —— diet —— factor —— speculation ——.

—— present —— ethnic —— mix —— 90 percent —— Kochenese —— 5 percent —— Chinese —— 5 percent —— others —— including —— Europeans —— Americans ——.

NOTES

Popul^n—Kochen—'75 census 25 million

    Norkhan—5 mil.

    Norpin—1.5 mil.

    Sumalark—1 mil.

3 popl^n centers

Many small towns

    Hamlets: 5–10 thousand popl^n

        Buddhist temple in center

        Small group of shops

        Gov't office bldg

        No residential district

        People live nearby

        Bus service connecting to principal cities

Kochenese—Who are they?

    Resemble Thais, Burmese, Vietnamese

    Theory—mix of people from Indonesia, Malaysia & China. Mixed w/ indigenous

        tribes. Happened long time ago.

    Slightly taller than Thais. Why? Diet?

Ethnic mix—today

    90% K

    5% Chinese

    5% Europeans, Americans, etc.

YOUR NOTES

QUIZ

1. How many major population centers does Kochen have?

2. Describe a typical Kochenese hamlet.

3. What is the origin of the modern Kochenese according to one theory?

4. What reason was given for the height difference between the Kochenese and the Thais?

5. What is the ethnic mix of the population of Kochen?

QUIZ ANSWERS

1. How many major population centers does Kochen have?
   Three

2. Describe a typical Kochenese hamlet.
   Buddhist temple at the center, a government office building, and a small group of shops. No residential district. Villagers live nearby.

3. What is the origin of the modern Kochenese according to one theory?
   They are a mixture of peoples from Indonesia, Malaysia, and China with indigenous tribes.

4. What reason was given for the height difference between the Kochenese and the Thais?
   Diet

5. What is the ethnic mix of the population of Kochen?
   90% Kochenese
   5% Chinese
   5% Other—Europeans, Americans, etc.

Education (I)

READING PREPARATION

According to the lecturer, public education was brought to Kochen in 1874 after a trip abroad by the king, Popupat. The king made his decision after seeing the benefits of public education in other countries. Before 1874, the lecturer says, the temple schools carried on some kind of education but in a haphazard way. Members of the royal family received tutoring in the palace.

The lecturer says that Kochen today boasts one of the best educational systems in Southeast Asia. Evidently when the king decided to introduce public education to his country, he did so with a vengeance. He sought the aid of the Stoneman Foundation to assist in educating a corps of teachers. The lecturer notes that the king made a proposal to the Foundation involving the recruitment of teachers. For this, he would put up half the financial support. Stoneman bought his idea, and soon the first boat-load of American teachers came to Kochen. Next, bright, able young Kochenese were selected to be the teachers who would ultimately become the next generation's teacher-trainers. In order that these young teachers could absorb what the American teachers had to offer, they were given a crash course in English. On the other hand, the lecturer points out, King Popupat insisted, and wisely so, that the Americans be given intensive training in Kochenese. This learning of the two languages by both parties undoubtedly expedited the exchange of information. The lecturer says it is a shame that other areas seeking outside assistance haven't followed a like pattern.

The teachers sponsored by the Stoneman Foundation stayed eight years in Kochen and helped the Kochenese government set up three teacher-training colleges, one in each of the principal cities. In Norkhan, Popupat University was established. Today's main source of teachers for the elementary and secondary schools are the three teacher-training colleges. The lecturer concludes by saying that he'll continue discussing education next time.

DICTATION

1. _____   1. _____

2. _____   2. _____

3. _____   3. _____

4. _____   4. _____

5. _____   5. _____

6. _____   6. _____

7. _____   7. _____

8. _____   8. _____

9. _____   9. _____

10. _____   10. _____

11. _____   11. _____

12. _____   12. _____

13. _____   13. _____

14. _____   14. _____

15. _____   15. _____

16. _____   16. _____

17. _____   17. _____

18. _____   18. _____

19. _____   19. _____

20. _____   20. _____

21. _____   21. _____

22. _____   22. _____

23. _____   23. _____

24. _____   24. _____

25. _____   25. _____

Number correct _____

AUDING PROMPT A

Public education came to Kochen in 1874 following a trip abroad by the then ruling monarch, King Popupat. The king decided that his people should have the benefits of public education after seeing what other countries were doing. Until that time, education had been carried on in temple schools in a sort of haphazard way, and of course, members of the royal family were tutored in various subjects in the palace.

Today, Kochen boasts one of the best educational systems in all of Southeast Asia. When King Popupat decided to introduce public education to Kochen, he did so with a vengeance. His first move was to educate a corps of teachers and he did this by seeking the aid of the Stoneman Foundation. He proposed to the Foundation that if they would recruit the teacher-trainers, he would put up half the financial support needed. Stoneman bought the idea, and before long the first boat-load of American teachers arrived in Kochen. Bright, able young Kochenese were selected to be the teachers who would ultimately become the teacher-trainers of the next generation. These young teachers were given crash courses in English so that they could absorb what the teachers from America had to offer. Very wisely, King Popupat also insisted that the American teachers be given intensive training in Kochenese—a most unusual requirement. The learning of the two languages by the parties concerned certainly expedited the exchange of information. It's really a shame that other areas seeking outside help haven't followed a similar pattern.

The Stoneman Foundation–sponsored teachers remained in Kochen for eight years and assisted the Kochenese government in setting up three teacher-training colleges, one in each of the principal cities. Eventually, Popupat University was established in the capital city of Norkhan. The three teacher-training colleges are still going strong and are the main source of teachers for the kingdom's elementary and secondary schools. I'll have more to say next time about education.

AUDING PROMPT B

Public education came to Kochen in 1874 following _____ trip abroad by _____ _____ _____ _____, King Popupat. _____ king decided _____ _____ people should have _____ benefits of public education after seing what other countries were doing. Until that time, education had been _____ _____ in temple schools in _____ sort of haphazard way, _____ _____ _____, members of _____ royal family were tutored _____ _____ _____ in _____ palace.

Today, Kochen boasts one of _____ best educational systems in _____ _____ Southeast Asia. When _____ Popupat decided to introduce public education _____ _____, _____ did so with _____ vengeance. _____ first move _____ _____ educate _____ corps of teachers _____ _____ did this by seeking _____ aid of _____ Stoneman Foundation. _____ proposed to _____ Foundation _____ if they would recruit _____ teacher-trainers, he would put up half _____ financial support _____. Stoneman bought _____ idea, _____ before long _____ first boat-load of American teachers arrived _____ _____. Bright, able young Kochenese _____ selected to be _____ teachers who would ultimately become _____ teacher-trainers of _____ next generation. _____ _____ teachers were given crash courses in English so _____ they could absorb what _____ teachers from America had to offer. _____ _____, _____ Popupat _____ insisted _____ _____ American teachers be given intensive training in Kochenese—_____ _____ _____ _____. _____ learning of the two languages _____ _____ _____ _____ _____ expedited _____ exchange of information. _____ _____ _____ shame _____ other areas seeking outside help haven't followed _____ similar pattern.

_____ Stoneman Foundation–sponsored teachers remained in Kochen eight years _____ assisted _____ Kochenese government in setting up three teacher-training colleges, _____ in each of _____ principal cities. _____, Popupat University _____ established in _____ _____ _____ _____ Norkhan. _____ _____ teacher-training colleges _____ still going strong _____ are _____ main source of teachers for _____ _____ elementary and secondary schools. _____ _____ more to say next time about education.

AUDING PROMPT C

—— public —— education —— came —— Kochen —— 1874 —— following —— trip —— abroad —— King Popupat ——. —— king —— decided —— people —— have —— benefits —— public —— education —— after —— seeing —— other —— countries —— doing ——. —— education —— had —— been —— temple. —— schools —— haphazard —— way —— members —— royal —— family —— tutored —— palace ——.

—— today —— Kochen —— boasts —— best —— educational —— systems —— Southeast Asia ——. —— Popupat —— decided —— introduce —— public —— education —— did —— with —— vengeance ——. —— first —— move —— educate —— corps —— teachers —— seeking —— aid —— Stoneman Foundation ——. —— proposed —— Foundation —— if —— would —— recruit —— teacher-trainers —— he —— put up —— half —— financial —— support ——. —— Stoneman —— bought —— idea —— before —— long —— first —— boat-load —— American —— teachers —— arrived ——. —— bright —— able —— young —— Kochenese —— selected —— to —— be —— teachers —— ultimately —— become —— teacher-trainers —— next —— generation ——. —— teachers —— given —— crash —— courses —— English —— so —— could —— absorb —— what —— teachers —— America —— offer ——. —— Popupat —— insisted —— American —— teachers —— given —— intensive —— training —— Kochenese ——. —— learning —— two —— languages —— expedited ——

exchange —— information ——. —— shame —— other —— areas —— seeking —— help —— haven't —— followed —— similar —— pattern ——.
—— Stoneman —— teachers —— remained —— Kochen —— eight —— years —— assisted —— government —— setting —— up —— three —— teacher-training —— colleges —— each —— principal —— cities ——. —— Popupat University —— established —— Norkhan ——. —— teacher-training —— colleges —— still —— going —— strong —— main —— source —— teachers —— elementary —— secondary —— schools ——.

NOTES

Public educ^n —1874

    Followed trip abroad by King Popupat

    King P decided subjects should have benefits of pub. educ^n

Before 1874

    Educ^n in temple schools—haphazard

    Royal family tutored in palace

Today

    Kochen—one of best in S.E.A.

    King P went to Stoneman Fdn

        Proposal: Fdn recruit teachers, Kochen put up 1/2 $

            Stoneman accepted—sent teachers

    Bright, able young Ks selected to be future teacher-trainers

        Given crash course in Eng. so could learn from Americans

        King insisted Amer. learn Kochenese! Unusual for the time

        Lang. learning facilitated xchange of info

Stoneman teachers stayed 8 yrs

    Set up 3 teacher-tng colleges—in 3 prin. cities

    Popupat Univ estab. in Norkhan

    Teacher-tng college main source of t's for elem & sec schools

YOUR NOTES

QUIZ

1. Explain how public education came to be introduced to Kochen.

2. How would you rank the educational system of Kochen compared with those of other countries in Southeast Asia?

3. Whom did King Popupat turn to for financial assistance?

4. What were the terms that King Popupat came to with the source of financial aid in (3)?

5. How long did the American teachers stay in Kochen?

6. How many teacher-training institutions were established as a result of the agreement?

QUIZ ANSWERS

1. Explain how public education came to be introduced to Kochen.
   King Popupat went abroad in 1874 and after seeing public education in other countries decided to introduce it to Kochen.

2. How would you rank the educational system of Kochen compared with those of other countries in Southeast Asia?
   One of the best.

3. Whom did King Popupat turn to for financial assistance?
   The Stoneman Foundation.

4. What were the terms that King Popupat came to with the source of financial aid in (3)?
   If the Foundation would recruit the teachers, Kochen would put up half the money. American teachers had to take intensive training in Kochenese.

5. How long did the American teachers stay in Kochen?
   8 years.

6. How many teacher-training institutions were established as a result of the agreement?
   Three.

Education (II)

READING PREPARATION

The lecturer continues with the subject of education. He recalls that he mentioned last time that the Stoneman Foundation had given assistance to the Kochenese government in the education field. Also, the Foundation was involved with the school of medicine. He says that he will talk about the medical school in his lecture on public health.

According to the lecturer, the system of education in Kochen follows a similar pattern to that found in the United States. There are four years of elementary school, two of middle school, three of junior high school, and three of senior high school. This gives a total of twelve years. Most Kochenese complete high school, although education is compulsory only through the ninth grade. In farming areas, however, some of the children leave school following completion of the ninth grade and begin careers in farming. In the main cities of the kingdom—i.e., Norkhan, Norpin, and Sumalark—close to 90 percent of the children finish high school.

The next topic is enrollment figures in Popupat University and the three teacher-training colleges. Citing the 1975 figures, he gives the following: Norkhan, 7,500; Norpin, 4,000; Sumalark, 3,500; and at the university almost 10,000. The approximate total is 25,000. To this total must be added the enrollment of the medical school, a separate institution, which comes to about 200 students. This medical school, named for the queen's father, is called Praching Medical School and Hospital. The grand total of those in higher education at any one time is a little over 25,000.

The lecturer mentions that Popupat University is divided into three colleges: agriculture, engineering, and arts and sciences. Of the three colleges, he points out that agriculture is by far the largest.

DICTATION

1. _____	1. _____
2. _____	2. _____
3. _____	3. _____
4. _____	4. _____
5. _____	5. _____
6. _____	6. _____
7. _____	7. _____
8. _____	8. _____
9. _____	9. _____
10. _____	10. _____
11. _____	11. _____
12. _____	12. _____
13. _____	13. _____
14. _____	14. _____
15. _____	15. _____
16. _____	16. _____
17. _____	17. _____
18. _____	18. _____
19. _____	19. _____
20. _____	20. _____
21. _____	21. _____

22. _____   22. _____

23. _____   23. _____

24. _____   24. _____

25. _____   25. _____

Number correct _____

AUDING PROMPT A

I want to continue today with the subject of education in Kochen. I mentioned last time that the Stoneman Foundation had assisted the Kochenese government in the field of education. In addition to this, the Foundation also was involved with the medical school. I won't go into that today, but will cover it when I talk about public health a little later on.

The educational system in Kochen follows a pattern somewhat similar to that which we find in the United States. Basically, there are four years of elementary school, two years of middle, three years of junior high, and three years of senior high. That makes a total of twelve years. Now, education is compulsory through the ninth grade, but as a matter of fact, most Kochenese finish high school. In some of the more rural areas, some of the kids leave school after the ninth grade and go to work on the farms. In Norkhan, Norpin, and Sumalark, on the other hand—in other words in the principal cities of Kochen—we find close to 90 percent of the children finishing high school.

How many go on to Popupat University? Actually, I should ask how many go on to the three teacher-training colleges and the university. The enrollment in the three teacher-training colleges in 1975 was as follows: In Norkhan, the enrollment was 7,500; in Norpin, 4,000; in Sumalark, 3,500; and at the university almost 10,000. This gives us a rough total of 25,000 all told. The other institute of higher education is, of course, the medical school, which is separate from Popupat University. Praching Medical School and Hospital, named for the queen's father, has an enrollment of just under 200 students. Thus we have just over 25,000 in pursuit of higher education at any one time.

Popupat University has three colleges: agriculture, engineering, and arts and sciences, with agriculture being by far the largest. See you next time.

AUDING PROMPT B

_____ _____ _____ continue _____ with _____ subject of education in Kochen. I mentioned _____ _____ _____ _____ Stoneman Foundation had assisted _____ Kochenese government in _____ _____ _____ education. In addition _____ _____, _____ Foundation also _____ involved with _____ medical school. _____ _____ _____ _____ _____ _____, _____ will cover it when I talk about public health _____ _____ later _____.

_____ educational system in Kochen follows _____ pattern _____ similar to _____ _____ _____ _____ _____ _____ United States. _____, _____ _____ four years _____ elementary school, two _____ _____ middle, three _____ _____ junior high, _____ three _____ _____ senior high. _____ _____ _____ total of twelve years. _____, education is compulsory through _____ ninth grade, _____ _____ _____ _____ _____ _____, most Kochenese finish high school. In some _____ _____ more rural areas, some _____ _____ _____ leave school after _____ ninth grade _____ go to work on _____ farms. In Norkhan, Norpin, and Sumalark, _____ _____ _____ _____ _____—_____ _____ _____ _____ _____ _____ _____ _____ _____ _____ _____ _____

_____ _____ — _____ _____ close to 90 percent _____ _____ _____ finishing high school.

How many go _____ to Popupat University? _____ , I should ask how many go _____ to the three teacher-training colleges and _____ university. _____ enrollment in _____ three teacher-training colleges in 1975 was _____ _____ : _____ Norkhan, _____ _____ _____ 7,500; _____ Norpin, 4,000; _____ Sumalark, 3,500; and at _____ university almost 10,000. _____ gives _____ _____ rough total of 25,000 _____ _____ . _____ other institute of higher education is, _____ _____ , _____ medical school, which is separate from Popupat University. Praching Medical School and Hospital, named for _____ queen's father, has _____ enrollment _____ just under 200 _____ . Thus _____ _____ just over 25,000 in pursuit of higher education _____ _____ _____ _____ .

Popupat University has three colleges: agriculture, engineering, _____ arts and sciences, with agriculture _____ _____ _____ the largest. _____ _____ _____ _____ .

AUDING PROMPT C

—— continue —— subject —— education —— Kochen ——. —— mentioned —— Stoneman Foundation —— assisted —— Kochenese —— government —— education ——. —— Foundation —— also —— involved —— medical —— school ——. —— cover —— it —— when —— I —— talk —— about —— public —— health ——.

—— educational —— system —— follows —— pattern —— similar —— United States ——. —— four —— years —— elementary —— two —— middle —— three —— junior —— high —— three —— senior —— high ——. —— total —— twelve —— years ——. —— education —— compulsory —— through —— ninth —— grade —— most —— Kochenese —— finish —— high —— school ——. —— some —— rural —— areas —— some —— leave —— school —— after —— ninth —— grade —— work —— on —— farms ——. —— Norkhan —— Norpin —— Sumalark —— close —— to —— 90 —— percent —— finishing —— high —— school ——.

—— how —— many —— go —— Popupat —— University ——? —— how —— many —— go —— three —— teacher-training —— colleges —— and —— university ——. —— enrollment —— three —— teacher-training —— colleges —— 1975 —— Norkhan —— 7,500 —— Norpin —— 4,000 —— Sumalark —— 3,500 —— university —— almost —— 10,000 ——. —— rough —— total —— 25,000 ——. —— other —— institute —— higher —— education —— is —— medical —— school —— separate —— Popupat —— University ——. —— Praching —— Medical —— School —— and —— Hospital —— named —— queen's —— father —— enrollment —— just —— under —— 200 ——. —— just —— over —— 25,000 —— in —— pursuit —— higher —— education ——.

—— Popupat —— University —— three —— colleges —— agriculture —— engineering —— arts and sciences —— agriculture —— largest ——.

NOTES

Educⁿ—cont.

Stoneman—support for med. school

Educⁿ system—similar to U.S.

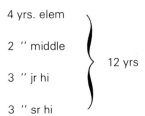

4 yrs. elem

2 " middle

3 " jr hi   12 yrs

3 " sr hi

Compulsory—thru 9th grd

Most Ko. finish hi school

Rural area—some lv after 9th & work on farms

Norkhan, Norpin, Sumalark—90% finish hi sch.

Popupat Univ & TT Colleges

1975—Norkhan 7,500

Norpin 4,000

Sumalark 3,500   25,000

Univ 10,000

Praching Med Sch & Hosp (named for queen's dad)

200 Ss

Popupat U—3 colleges

Ag—biggest

Engr

A&S

YOUR NOTES

QUIZ

1. Through what grade level is education compulsory in Kochen?

2. How do the rural and urban areas of Kochen differ with respect to the total amount of education completed?

3. How many institutes of higher education does Kochen have? List them.

4. What are the colleges which constitute the university? Which of these has the largest enrollment?

QUIZ ANSWERS

1. Through what grade level is education compulsory in Kochen?
   Ninth

2. How do the rural and urban areas of Kochen differ with respect to the total amount of education completed?
   Rural—some students finish only ninth grade and then work on farms.
   Urban—about 90 percent finish high school.

3. How many institutes of higher education does Kochen have? List them.
   5—Popupat University
      Norkhan Teacher-Training College
      Norpin Teacher-Training College
      Sumalark Teacher-Training College
      Praching Medical School & Hospital

4. What are the colleges which constitute the university? Which of these has the largest enrollment?
   Agriculture (largest)
   Engineering
   Arts & Sciences

Public Health (I)

READING PREPARATION

The lecturer begins by saying that the Kochenese, on the whole, are a reasonably healthy group of people. In the cities, he says, the people have access to medical facilities which are quite good. However, those who reside in rural areas have more health problems.

The common tropical diseases which the Kochenese are subject to are cholera, amebic dysentery, typhoid fever, typhus, and Hansen's disease (leprosy). Bubonic plague used to be a problem, but is now under control, according to the lecturer. Other diseases include smallpox, tuberculosis, dengue fever, yaws (now under control through the use of penicillin), and malaria.

The lecturer states that Kochen has a good public health service, although there aren't enough doctors out in the countryside. The reason for this, he says, is that most of the doctors want to stay in the cities and make money.

He continues that before Kochen had its own medical school, students went abroad, to France and England for the most part, to study. Some went to the United States. Only the sons of the wealthy could afford this because this kind of education is very expensive.

The Stoneman Foundation in the U.S. was approached by the queen. Working in concert with some Kochenese physicians, she asked for its assistance in establishing a four-year medical college. This was in 1935. The whole concept, the lecturer notes, was based on a reciprocal principle: the Kochenese would supply the land, buildings, and staff housing for American staff. Also, the Kochenese agreed to support four visiting professors interested in tropical medicine for a ten-year period. In addition to this, the Kochenese said they would support four residents.

DICTATION

1. _____	1. _____
2. _____	2. _____
3. _____	3. _____
4. _____	4. _____
5. _____	5. _____
6. _____	6. _____
7. _____	7. _____
8. _____	8. _____
9. _____	9. _____
10. _____	10. _____
11. _____	11. _____
12. _____	12. _____
13. _____	13. _____
14. _____	14. _____
15. _____	15. _____
16. _____	16. _____
17. _____	17. _____
18. _____	18. _____
19. _____	19. _____
20. _____	20. _____
21. _____	21. _____

22. _____   22. _____

23. _____   23. _____

24. _____   24. _____

25. _____   25. _____

Number correct _____

AUDING PROMPT A

The people of Kochen are a reasonably healthy lot, taking the population as a whole. The people in the cities have access to good medical facilities, but those in the rural areas are subject to more health problems. I'll expand on this a little later.

The Kochenese suffer from the common tropical diseases such as cholera, amebic dysentery, typhoid fever, some typhus, and Hansen's disease, or as it is more commonly known, leprosy. Let's see, what else? At one time bubonic plague was a problem, but it's been brought under control quite well. There are smallpox and tuberculosis, of course. In addition, we find dengue fever, some yaws (although this has been pretty much wiped out through the use of penicillin), and let's not forget malaria.

Kochen has a rather good public health service. While there aren't enough doctors out in the countryside—you know, it's the age-old problem: most of the doctors want to stay in the cities and get rich—still there's a pretty good public health program.

In the days before Kochen had a medical school, students went abroad, primarily to France and England and to a lesser degree to the United States, to study medicine. Needless to say this was expensive education and only the sons of the wealthy could afford this kind of training.

In 1935, the queen, working in concert with a group of Kochenese doctors, approached the Stoneman Foundation in the U.S. and asked for its assistance in setting up a four-year medical school. The idea was based on a reciprocal principle: on their part, the Kochenese would provide the land, buildings, etc. for a medical college. Also, the Kochenese would supply housing for staff from the States. In addition to this, the Kochenese agreed to support four visiting professors interested in the problems of tropical medicine for a period of ten years along with four assistants, doctors at the resident level. I see my time is up. More later on this.

AUDING PROMPT B

_____ people of Kochen are _____ reasonably healthy lot, taking _____ population as _____ whole. _____ people in _____ cities have access to good medical facilities, but those in _____ rural areas _____ subject to more health problems. _____ _____ _____ _____ _____ _____ _____.

_____ Kochenese suffer from _____ common tropical diseases _____ _____ cholera, amebic dysentery, typhoid fever, _____ typhus, and Hansen's disease, _____ as _____ _____ _____ commonly known, leprosy. _____ _____, _____ _____? _____ one time bubonic plague was _____ problem, but _____ _____ brought under control quite well. _____ _____ smallpox and tuberculosis, _____ _____. _____ _____, _____ _____ dengue fever, some yaws (although

_____ _____ _____ pretty much wiped out through _____ _____ _____ penicillin), _____ _____ _____ _____ malaria.

Kochen has _____ rather good public health service. _____ _____ aren't enough doctors _____ in _____ countryside—_____ _____, _____ _____ age-old problem: most _____ _____ doctors want to stay in _____ cities and get rich!— _____ _____ a pretty good public health program.

_____ _____ _____ before Kochen had _____ medical school, students went abroad, primarily to France _____ England _____ to _____ lesser degree _____ the United States, to study _____. _____ _____ _____ _____ was expensive education _____ only _____ sons of _____ wealthy could afford _____ _____ _____ training.

_____ 1935, _____ queen, _____ in concert with _____ group of Kochenese doctors, approached _____ Stoneman Foundation in _____ U.S. _____ asked for _____ assistance in setting up _____ four-year medical school. _____ idea _____ based on _____ reciprocal principle: _____ _____ _____, _____ Kochenese would provide _____ land, buildings, _____ for _____ medical college. _____, _____ Kochenese would supply housing for staff from _____ States. _____ _____ _____ _____, _____ Kochenese agreed to support four visiting professors interested in _____ _____ _____ tropical medicine for _____ _____ _____ ten years along with four assistants, _____ at _____ resident level. _____ _____ _____ _____ _____ _____. _____ _____ _____ _____.

AUDING PROMPT C

—— people —— Kochen —— reasonably —— healthy —— taking —— population —— as —— whole ——. —— people —— cities —— access —— good —— medical —— facilities —— rural —— areas —— subject —— to —— health —— problems ——.

—— Kochenese —— suffer —— common —— tropical —— diseases —— cholera —— amebic dysentery —— typhoid fever —— typhus —— Hansen's disease —— leprosy ——. —— one —— time —— bubonic plague —— problem —— but —— under —— control ——. —— smallpox —— tuberculosis ——. —— dengue fever —— yaws —— wiped —— out —— penicillin —— malaria ——.

—— Kochen —— good —— public —— health —— service ——. —— aren't —— enough —— doctors —— countryside —— old —— problem —— most —— doctors —— want —— stay —— cities —— get —— rich —— pretty —— good —— public —— health —— program ——.

—— before —— Kochen —— medical —— school —— students —— abroad —— primarily —— France —— England —— lesser —— degree —— United States ——. —— expensive —— education —— only —— sons —— wealthy —— afford ——.

—— 1935 —— queen —— concert —— Kochenese —— doctors —— approached —— Stoneman —— Foundation —— U.S. —— asked —— assistance —— setting —— up —— four-year —— medical —— school ——. —— idea —— based —— reciprocal —— principle —— Kochenese —— provide —— land —— buildings —— supply —— housing —— staff —— States ——. —— Kochenese —— support —— four —— visiting —— professors —— interested —— tropical —— medicine —— for —— ten —— years —— with —— four —— assistants —— resident —— level ——.

NOTES

Public health

    Kochenese—reasonably healthy popln

    Cities—good medical facilities; rural, not so good

Common trop. diseases—

    cholera, amb. dys., typhoid, typhus, Hansen's disease, bubonic plague (now

        under control), smallpox, I.B., dengue, yaws (pencillin controlled), malaria

Good public health serv.

    Not enough doctors in sticks—stay in cities for $

Before med school

    Ss to Eng. & France—expensive, wealthy kids only

1935—queen + group of doctors asked Stoneman Fdn for $

    Kochenese to supply: land, bldgs, staff housing, support 4 visiting profs (for 10

        yrs) interested in trop. med., also 4 residents

YOUR NOTES

QUIZ

1. Contrast the medical facilities in the urban and rural areas of Kochen.

2. Name five diseases which are found in Kochen.

3. Where do most doctors prefer to practice medicine and why?

4. Where were Kochenese medical personnel trained before the establishment of the medical school?

5. When the idea for a medical school was proposed in 1935, what were the Kochenese asked to provide?

QUIZ ANSWERS

1. Contrast the medical facilities in the urban and rural areas of Kochen.
   City people have access to better medical facilities than do country people.

2. Name five diseases which are found in Kochen.
   Cholera, amebic dysentery, typhoid fever, typhus, leprosy (bubonic plague, smallpox, tuberculosis, dengue fever, yaws, malaria)

3. Where do most doctors prefer to practice medicine and why?
   In the cities. There is more money to be made in the cities.

4. Where were Kochenese medical personnel trained before the establishment of the medical school?
   France, England, and the United States.

5. When the idea for a medical school was proposed in 1935, what were the Kochenese asked to provide?
   Land, buildings, housing, support for four professors and four residents for a 10-year period.

Public Health (II)

READING PREPARATION

The lecturer says that he will now finish his discussion of the relationship between the Stoneman Foundation and Praching Medical School. He notes that the Foundation was requested to furnish a cadre of American professors of medicine for a four-year period, with the total number of Americans coming to a maximum of fifteen. He remarks that very few of the teachers stayed longer than two years because they had academic responsibilities at home. Finally, he says that an average of ten to twelve American doctors were teaching at any one time.

The lecturer notes that one of the major costs was the construction of a teaching hospital. He comments that the queen and her advisors used their heads: instead of building a big concrete building, they built facilities appropriate to the Kochenese style of living. He describes the buildings as one-story, open, and airy, suitable for the climate. Another feature of the hospital–medical school complex, he says, is facilities for family members to stay with the patients. This contrasts with the American situation where patients are rather isolated from their families, who are permitted to visit only during specified times. He points out that hospitals in the United States are strict about this, although lately there has been a relaxation of restrictions. The Kochenese situation is different because families would feel as if they were deserting their relatives if they left them alone in hospitals. The Kochenese hospital has sleeping and cooking facilities in most of the rooms. Patients with communicable diseases are isolated, the lecturer says.

This kind of construction and arrangement spreads the hospital facilities over a considerable area, so the medical school is a rather sprawling structure. This arrangement forces the nurses and doctors to walk considerable distances at times, but it does provide patient comfort and this is the function of the hospital.

DICTATION

1. _____   1. _____

2. _____   2. _____

3. _____   3. _____

4. _____   4. _____

5. _____   5. _____

6. _____   6. _____

7. _____   7. _____

8. _____   8. _____

9. _____   9. _____

10. _____   10. _____

11. _____   11. _____

12. _____   12. _____

13. _____   13. _____

14. _____   14. _____

15. _____   15. _____

16. _____   16. _____

17. _____   17. _____

18. _____   18. _____

19. _____   19. _____

20. _____   20. _____

21. _____   21. _____

22. _____   22. _____

23. _____   23. _____

24. _____   24. _____

25. _____   25. _____

Number correct _____

AUDING PROMPT A

Let's see, I was just about to finish discussing the relationship between the Stoneman Foundation and Praching Med School. Now, the Stoneman Foundation was asked to supply a cadre of American professors of medicine for four years, and the total number of American professors came to fifteen at the maximum. Very few of these teachers stayed more than two years at a time because of other academic commitments back home. On the average ten to twelve American doctors were teaching at any one time.

One of the major costs was, obviously, the building of a teaching hospital. However, the queen and her advisors really used their noodles here. Instead of building a big concrete hospital building, they built hospital facilities more in keeping with the Kochenese life style. Most of the buildings are one-story, very open and airy—really quite suitable for Kochen's climate. Another feature of the hospital–medical school complex was facilities for families, or at least a family representative, to stay with the patient. As you know, in the U.S. patients are pretty much isolated from their families except for rather rigidly enforced visiting hours. There is a little loosening up of this restriction, but for the most part, I think hospitals are fairly strict about these things. In Kochen, it's another story. Families would feel as if they were deserting their relations if they left them in a hospital all alone. So, there are sleeping facilities and even cooking facilities in most of the rooms. Of course, patients with communicable diseases, are isolated.

With this sort of arrangement the hospital presents a sprawling appearance—that is, it's spread out all over the place. After all, hospitals are for the comfort of patients, so if the nurses and doctors have to walk some distance it's no big problem. Probably good exercise for them!

AUDING PROMPT B

_____ _____, _____ _____ _____ _____ _____ finish discussing _____ relationship between _____ Stoneman Foundation and Praching Med School. _____, _____ Stoneman Foundation _____ asked to supply _____ cadre _____ American professors of medicine for four years, _____ _____ total number _____ American professors _____ _____ fifteen _____ _____ maximum. Very few _____ _____ _____ stayed more than two years _____ _____ _____ because of other academic commitments _____ _____. On _____ average ten to twelve American doctors _____ teaching at _____ one time.

One of _____ major costs was, _____, _____ building of _____ teaching hospital. However, _____ queen and _____ advisors _____ used their noodles _____. Instead of building _____ big concrete hospital building, _____ built _____ facilities more in keeping with _____ Kochenese life style. Most _____ _____ buildings _____ one-story, very open and airy—_____ _____ suitable for

_____ climate. Another feature of the hospital–medical school complex was facilities for families, or _____ _____ _____ family representative, to stay with the patient. _____ _____ _____, in _____ U.S. patients _____ pretty much isolated from _____ families except for rather rigidly enforced visiting hours. _____ is _____ little loosening up _____ _____ _____, but _____ _____ _____ _____ , _____ _____ hospitals are fairly strict _____ _____ _____. In Kochen, _____ another story. Families would feel as if _____ _____ deserting their relations if _____ left them in _____ hospital _____ alone. _____, there are sleeping facilities _____ _____ cooking facilities in most _____ _____ rooms. _____ _____, patients with communicable diseases _____ isolated.

With this _____ _____ arrangement _____ hospital presents _____ sprawling appearance—_____ _____, _____ _____ _____ _____ _____ _____ _____. _____ _____, hospitals are for _____ comfort of patients, _____ if _____ nurses and doctors have to walk some distance _____ no big problem. _____ _____ _____ _____ _____!

AUDING PROMPT C

—— finish —— discussing —— relationship —— Stoneman Foundation —— Praching Med School ——. —— Stoneman Foundation —— asked —— supply —— cadre —— American —— professors —— medicine —— four —— years —— total —— professors —— fifteen —— maximum ——. —— very —— few —— stayed —— more —— than —— two —— years —— because —— academic —— commitments ——. —— average —— ten —— twelve —— American —— doctors —— teaching —— one —— time ——.

—— one —— major —— costs —— building —— teaching —— hospital ——. —— queen —— advisors —— used —— noodles ——. —— instead of —— concrete —— buildings ——built —— facilities —— in keeping —— Kochenese —— life —— style ——. —— most —— buildings —— one-story —— open —— airy —— suitable —— for —— climate ——. —— another —— feature —— hospital–medical school —— facilities —— for —— families —— stay —— with —— patient ——. —— U.S. —— patients —— isolated —— from —— families —— except —— rigidly —— enforced —— visiting —— hours ——. —— loosening up —— but —— hospitals —— strict ——. —— Kochen —— another —— story ——. —— families —— would —— feel —— deserting —— relations —— if —— left —— them —— hospital —— alone ——. —— sleeping —— facilities —— cooking —— facilities —— most —— rooms ——. —— patients —— with —— communicable —— diseases —— isolated ——.

—— this —— arrangement —— hospital —— presents —— sprawling ——. —— hospitals —— for —— comfort —— patients —— if —— nurses —— doctors —— walk —— distance —— no —— problem ——.

NOTES

Public health—cont.

Stoneman Fdn & Praching Med School

S.F.—supplied Amer. prof of med for 4 yrs

Total = 15 max. at one time

Avg stay = 2 yrs

Avg 10–12 Amer doctors teaching at one time

Hospital facilities

Adapted to Kochenese life style—mostly one-story, open, airy

Family facilities (live-in) provided—cooking/sleeping

Contrasts w/ U.S. conditions—patients alone, fairly strict visiting hours

Hospital is spread out = doctors & nurses must walk

YOUR NOTES

QUIZ

1. Describe briefly the design of the hospital facilities at Praching Medical
   School.

2. What are the significant differences between the U.S. and Kochen concerning patient–family relationships in hospital situations?

3. How does the patient–family relationship for patients with communicable
   diseases differ from that of other patients?

QUIZ ANSWERS

1. Describe briefly the design of the hospital facilities at Praching Medical School.

   Most buildings are one-story and are open and well-ventilated, making them suitable for Kochen's climate.

2. What are the significant differences between the U.S. and Kochen concerning patient–family relationships in hospital situations?

   In the U.S. families may visit patients only during regularly scheduled visiting hours, whereas in Kochen family members can stay with the patients in the hospital rooms. In fact, family members even do cooking for the Kochenese patients.

3. How does the patient–family relationship for patients with communicable diseases differ from that of other patients?

   Patients with communicable diseases are isolated whereas other patients have open contact with their families.

Religion

READING PREPARATION

According to the lecturer, Buddhism is the principal religion of Kochen, as it is in Thailand. Some 80 percent of the Kochenese are Buddhists, with the other 20 percent divided among Christians and minor sects of various kinds. Thus, he says, there are considerably more Christians in Kochen than in neighboring Thailand.

He continues that Buddhism came to Kochen from India in the early part of the sixth century. Before this, he says, the Kochenese were mostly animists. Some aspects of that belief remain to this day.

Buddhism was readily accepted by the Kochenese, he notes, and before long spread throughout the kingdom. Buddhist priests organized temple schools, the first regular schools. Today, the lecturer says, some of these schools still exist in the most rural parts of Kochen which are not yet adequately served by the Ministry of Education.

The lecturer remarks that most young men become monks for a three-month period some time during their lives, usually around age nineteen or twenty. There is a more or less permanent clergy composed of those who enter the monkhood early in life and remain in it. There is, however, rather fluid and flexible entry into and exit from the Buddhist priesthood.

The other strong religious influence is Christianity. The first Christians were Catholic priests from France who obtained permission to establish a church in Norkhan in 1830. Not long after this, the American Presbyterian Church arrived and established its mission. For several years, neither group made much headway in converting people. The Presbyterians, he says, in 1875 opened a school in Norkhan and taught subjects in English which drew certain parts of the population. For example, nobles of the court sent their children and soon others of the upper classes followed suit. The presence of children in their schools enhanced the chances of the missionaries to make converts.

DICTATION

1. _____

2. _____

3. _____

4. _____

5. _____

6. _____

7. _____

8. _____

9. _____

10. _____

11. _____

12. _____

13. _____

14. _____

15. _____

16. _____

17. _____

18. _____

19. _____

20. _____

21. _____

1. _____

2. _____

3. _____

4. _____

5. _____

6. _____

7. _____

8. _____

9. _____

10. _____

11. _____

12. _____

13. _____

14. _____

15. _____

16. _____

17. _____

18. _____

19. _____

20. _____

21. _____

22. _____   22. _____

23. _____   23. _____

24. _____   24. _____

25. _____   25. _____

Number correct _____

AUDING PROMPT A

The principal religion of Kochen is, like neighboring Thailand, Buddhism. Roughly 80 percent of the Kochenese are Buddhists, and the other 20 percent are divided among Christianity and various minor sects. There are considerably more Christians in Kochen than in Thailand.

Buddhism came to Kochen from India in the early part of the sixth century. Prior to this, the Kochenese were mostly animists, and some aspects of animism hang on to this day.

The Kochenese accepted Buddhism readily and the religion soon spread throughout the country. For all practical purposes, the first schools of any consequence were the schools organized by the priests in the temples. Some of these temple schools still exist in the most remote rural areas which are not yet adequately served by the Ministry of Education.

Most young males in the kingdom become monks for a period of three months in their lives. Usually, this happens around age nineteen or twenty. There is, of course, a cadre of more or less permanent clergy who enter the priesthood fairly early in life and stay in it for their entire adult life. However, exit from and entry into the Buddhist priesthood are rather fluid and flexible.

The other strong religious influence is Christianity. The first Christians to gain a foothold in Kochen were the Catholics, with priests from France gaining permission to establish a church in Norkhan in 1830. Shortly after this, a mission from the Presbyterian Church in America arrived to establish its mission, but for several years, neither church group made much headway in getting converts. Then, in 1875, the Presbyterians opened a school in Norkhan which presented the Kochenese with a chance to study English, and this was a strong attraction to certain segments of the population. Several nobles of the court sent their children to the school, and others of the upper classes soon followed suit. Once the missionaries had children in school their chances of converting some of the Kochenese to Christianity were enhanced.

AUDING PROMPT B

_____ principal religion of Kochen is, like _____ Thailand, Buddhism. Roughly 80 percent _____ _____ Kochenese are Buddhists, _____ _____ other 20 percent _____ divided among Christianity and various minor sects. _____ _____ considerably more Christians in Kochen than _____ Thailand.

Buddhism came to Kochen from India _____ _____ early part of _____ sixth century. Prior _____ _____, _____ Kochenese _____ mostly animists, _____ some aspects of animism hang on _____ _____ _____.

_____ Kochenese accepted Buddhism readily _____ the religion soon spread throughout _____ _____. _____ _____ _____ _____, _____ first schools of any consequence were _____ schools organized by _____ priests in _____ temples. Some ____ ____ temple schools still exist in ____ most remote rural areas ____ ____ not yet adequately served by ____ Ministry of Education.

Most young males ____ ____ ____ become monks for ____ ____ ____ three months ____ ____ ____. Usually, ____ happens ____ age nineteen or twenty. ____ ____, ____ ____, ____ cadre of more or less permanent clergy who enter ____ priesthood fairly early in life ____ stay in ____ for ____ entire adult life. However, exit from and entry into ____ ____ priesthood ____ rather fluid and flexible.

____ other strong religious influence is Christianity. ____ first Christians ____ ____ ____ ____ in Kochen were ____ Catholics, with priests from France gaining permission to establish a church in Norkhan in 1830. Shortly after ____, ____ mission from ____ Presbyterian Church in America arrived ____ ____ ____ ____, but for several years, neither church group made ____ headway in getting converts. ____, in 1875, ____ Presbyterians opened a school in Norkhan which presented ____ Kochenese ____ ____ chance to study English, ____ this was ____ strong attraction to certain segments of ____ population. Several nobles ____ ____ ____ sent their children to ____ school, ____ others of ____ upper classes ____ followed suit. Once ____ missionaries had children in school their chances of converting some ____ ____ ____ ____ ____ were enhanced.

AUDING PROMPT C

—— principal —— religion —— Kochen —— like —— Thailand —— Buddhism ——. —— roughly —— 80 percent —— Buddhists —— 20 percent —— Christianity —— minor —— sects ——. —— considerably —— more —— Christians —— Kochen —— than —— Thailand ——.

——Buddhism —— came —— Kochen —— from —— India —— early —— part —— sixth century ——. —— prior —— Kochenese —— mostly —— animists —— some —— aspects —— hang on ——.

—— Kochenese —— accepted —— Buddhism —— readily —— religion —— soon —— spread —— throughout ——. —— first —— schools —— any —— consequence —— organized —— by —— priests ——. —— some —— temple —— schools —— exist —— remote —— rural —— areas —— not —— yet —— adequately —— served —— by —— Ministry of Education ——.

—— most —— young —— males —— become —— monks —— for —— three —— months ——. —— usually —— happens —— age —— nineteen —— twenty ——. —— cadre —— permanent —— clergy —— enter —— priesthood —— early —— in —— life —— stay —— in —— entire —— life ——. —— exit —— from —— entry —— into —— priesthood —— fluid —— flexible ——.

—— other —— strong —— religious —— influence —— Christianity ——.
—— first —— Christians —— Catholics —— priests —— France —— gaining
—— permission —— establish —— church —— Norkhan —— 1830 ——.
—— shortly —— after —— mission —— Presbyterian Church —— America
—— arrived —— for —— several —— years —— neither —— group ——
made —— headway —— getting —— converts ——. —— 1875 —— Presbyterians —— opened —— school —— Norkhan —— presented —— Kochenese
—— chance —— study —— English —— strong —— attraction —— certain
—— segments —— population ——. —— nobles —— sent —— their ——
children —— others —— upper —— classes —— followed ——. —— once
—— missionaries —— had —— children —— school —— chances —— converting —— enhanced ——.

NOTES

Religion

    Buddhism—principal (like Thailand)

    80% Buddhists

    20% Christianity, minor sects

    More Christians than in Thailand

Buddhism

    Fr. India—6th c.

    Before this were animists—still some today

    Accepted B. readily—soon spread

    1st schools in temples—some today, rural areas

    Young men become monks for 3 mos. @ 19 or 20

    Permanent clergy exists—enter young; entry into/exit from priesthood fluid

       and flexible

Christianity

    Catholics first—French priests estab. church in Norkhan—1830

    Presby. Church next

    Neither group made many converts

    1875—Presby. opened school—taught Eng.

       Nobles sent kids, upper classes also = better chance to make converts

YOUR NOTES

QUIZ

1. Name and place in order from earliest to latest the organized religions which came to Kochen.

2. What were the origins of the religions which came to Kochen? (Show religion and place of origin.)

3. What was the relation between religion and the schools?

4. Where was the first church established in Kochen?

5. What triggered increased conversion to Christianity?

QUIZ ANSWERS

1. Name and place in order from earliest to latest the organized religions which came to Kochen.
   1. Buddhism   2. Catholics   3. Presbyterians

2. What were the origins of the religions which came to Kochen? (Show religion and place of origin.)
   Buddhism—India
   Catholics—France
   Presbyterians—America (or U.S.)

3. What was the relation between religion and the schools?
   First Kochenese schools were organized and conducted in Buddhist temples.

4. Where was the first church established in Kochen?
   Norkhan

5. What triggered increased conversion to Christianity?
   Teaching of English by missionary schools.

Agricultural Disaster

READING PREPARATION

The lecturer states that in 1935, the Kingdom of Kochen experienced one of its most serious disasters. He reminds us that Kochen is economically dependent on one crop: rice. Rice is paramount, although other products are involved in Kochen's economy. Before 1935, he says, loss of productivity because of damage by insects was small, and there had been relatively little trouble with rice diseases. He points out that all agricultural economies are subject to insect problems, diseases of plants, weather fluctuations, etc.

In 1935, serious trouble began. The lecturer sets the stage for what happened. In 1934, the weather was relatively dry and crops were a little below normal because of the below-average rainfall coupled with a hot season having temperatures considerably below normal. Thus, there was a late harvest. In Thailand, the rice stem borer had been causing some trouble. This is an obnoxious insect pest which bores into the stem of the rice plant, causing it to fall over because of the weakened condition of the stalk. Because of the climatic conditions he has described, Kochen was vulnerable for trouble. A further complication was that there were no strict plant-quarantine regulations, and DDT and other powerful insecticides were not available in Kochen.

It is not clear how the rice stem borer migrated from Thailand to Kochen. The results of the attack, however, were catastrophic. The Ministry of Agriculture reported that some 75 percent of the rice crop was wiped out. However, the lecturer says that Kochen had had extremely good harvests two years before so there was no famine. Naturally, he points out, although nobody actually went hungry, the invasion of this insect caused an adverse effect on the economy.

DICTATION

1. _____   1. _____

2. _____   2. _____

3. _____   3. _____

4. _____   4. _____

5. _____   5. _____

6. _____   6. _____

7. _____   7. _____

8. _____   8. _____

9. _____   9. _____

10. _____   10. _____

11. _____   11. _____

12. _____   12. _____

13. _____   13. _____

14. _____   14. _____

15. _____   15. _____

16. _____   16. _____

17. _____   17. _____

18. _____   18. _____

19. _____   19. _____

20. _____   20. _____

21. _____   21. _____

22. _____   22. _____

23. _____   23. _____

24. _____   24. _____

25. _____   25. _____

Number correct _____

AUDING PROMPT A

In 1935, Kochen suffered one of the most serious disasters the kingdom has ever experienced. Bear in mind that economically Kochen is dependent on rice. Rice is its number one crop; while the economy of Kochen involves other products, rice is unquestionably king. Until 1935, Kochen had had relatively little trouble with rice diseases and loss of productivity due to insect damage. However, any agricultural economy is subject to problems of insects, plant diseases, fluctuations in the weather, and so forth.

To put it mildly, disaster struck in 1935. Let me set the stage. The year before had been a relatively dry year. Crops were a bit below normal because of the below-average rainfall and because the hot season had been comparatively cool. As a result, crops were harvested somewhat late. In neighboring Thailand, farmers had had some trouble with the rice stem borer, an insect which is well described by its name. This particularly obnoxious pest bores into the stem of the rice plant as it nears maturity and causes the plant to topple over because of the weakened stalk. Well, the climatic conditions—a relatively cool summer and below-average rainfall—made Kochen a sitting duck for trouble. In those days, strict plant-quarantine regulations were unheard of. Furthermore, DDT and other powerful insecticides hadn't reached Kochen yet.

How the rice stem borer migrated from Thailand to Kochen nobody knows for sure. Without going into detail, let me say that the results were devastating. Approximately 75 percent of the rice crop was destroyed according to statistics of the Ministry of Agriculture. Imagine three-quarters of a nation's most important crop being wiped out. Fortunately, Kochen had a surplus of rice from the extremely good harvest of two years before. If it hadn't been for that, Kochen would undoubtedly have experienced a famine. Actually, nobody went hungry, but there was an adverse effect on the economy.

AUDING PROMPT B

_____ 1935, Kochen suffered one of _____ most serious disasters _____ kingdom _____ ever experienced. _____ _____ _____ _____ economically Kochen _____ dependent on rice. _____ _____ its number one crop; _____ _____ economy of Kochen involves other products, rice is unquestionably king. Until 1935, Kochen had _____ relatively little trouble with rice diseases and loss of productivity due to insect damage. However, any agricultural economy is subject to problems of insects, plant diseases, fluctuations in _____ weather, _____ _____ _____ .

_____ _____ _____ _____ , disaster struck in 1935. _____ _____ set the stage. _____ year before had been _____ relatively dry year. Crops _____ _____ bit below normal because _____ _____ below-average rainfall _____ _____ _____ hot season _____ _____ comparatively cool. As a result, crops _____ harvested somewhat late. In _____ Thailand, _____ _____ _____ some trouble with _____ rice stem borer, an insect _____ _____ _____ described by its name. This particularly obnoxious pest bores into _____ stem of _____ rice plant as _____ nears maturity _____ causes _____ plant to topple over because of _____ weakened stalk. _____, _____ climatic conditions—_____ relatively cool summer _____ below-average rainfall—made Kochen a sitting duck for trouble. In those days, strict plant-quarantine regulations were unheard of. Furthermore, DDT and óther powerful insecticides hadn't reached Kochen _____.

How _____ rice stem borer migrated from Thailand to Kochen nobody knows _____ _____. _____ _____ _____ _____, let me say _____ _____ results were devastating. Approximately 75 percent of _____ rice crop _____ destroyed according to _____ _____ _____ Ministry of Agriculture. _____ three-quarters of a nation's most important crop _____ wiped out. Fortunately, Kochen had _____ surplus _____ rice from _____ extremely good harvest _____ two years before. If it hadn't been for that, Kochen would undoubtedly have experienced _____ famine. _____, nobody went hungry, but _____ _____ _____ adverse effect on _____ economy.

AUDING PROMPT C

—— 1935 —— Kochen —— suffered —— most —— serious —— disasters —— ever —— experienced ——. —— economically —— Kochen —— dependent —— rice ——. —— number —— one —— crop —— economy —— Kochen —— involves —— other —— products —— rice —— unquestionably —— king ——. —— until —— 1935 —— Kochen —— little —— trouble —— rice —— diseases —— and —— loss —— productivity —— due to —— insect —— damage ——. —— agricultural —— economy —— subject —— problems —— insects —— plant —— diseases —— fluctuations —— weather ——.

—— disaster —— struck —— 1935 ——. —— set —— stage ——. —— year —— before —— relatively —— dry ——. —— crops —— below —— normal —— because —— below-average —— rainfall —— hot season —— comparatively —— cool ——. —— crops —— harvested —— late ——. —— Thailand —— trouble —— with —— rice stem borer —— insect —— described —— by —— name ——. —— obnoxious —— pest —— bores —— stem —— rice plant —— nears —— maturity —— causes —— plant —— topple —— over ——. —— climatic —— conditions —— cool —— summer —— below-average —— rainfall —— made —— Kochen —— sitting duck —— trouble ——. —— those —— days —— strict —— plant-quarantine —— regulations —— unheard —— of ——. —— DDT —— other —— powerful —— insecticides —— hadn't —— reached —— Kochen ——.

—— how —— rice —— stem —— borer —— migrated —— from —— Thailand —— Kochen —— nobody —— knows ——. —— results —— dev-

astating ——. —— approximately —— 75 percent —— rice —— crop ——
destroyed ——. —— three-quarters —— nation's —— most —— important
—— crop —— wiped out ——. —— Kochen —— had —— surplus —— rice
—— extremely —— good —— harvest —— two —— years —— before ——.
—— if —— hadn't —— been —— for —— that —— Kochen —— have ——
experienced —— famine ——. —— nobody —— went —— hungry —— but
—— adverse —— effect —— economy ——.

NOTES

1935—serious agric disaster

Kochen—rice = #1 crop

   Pre-1935 little trouble w/ rice diseases, insect damage

Conditions

   1934—rel. dry year

         —below avg. rainfall

         —cool hot season

         —late harvest

         —Thailand—trouble w/ rice stem borer

            obnoxious pest, bores into stem, plant topples over (weakened stem)

         —no strict quarantine in those days

         —no DDT, other insecticides

Results of rice stem borer devastating

      75% of rice crop destroyed (Min of Ag stat.)

   But—Kochen had rice surplus, ∴ no famine

   Bad effect on K's economy

YOUR NOTES

QUIZ

1. Before 1935, what effect had plant diseases and insects had on Kochen's rice crop?

2. What was the source of the insect which caused the damage to Kochen's rice crop?

3. What method of control was used to combat the insect?
   ( ) DDT
   ( ) Powerful insecticides
   ( ) Strict plant quarantine
   ( ) Not stated

4. What is the name of the insect responsible for the agricultural catastrophe in 1935 in Kochen?

5. What percentage of the 1935 rice crop was destroyed?

6. Describe the conditions which made Kochen a "sitting duck" for the 1935 trouble.

QUIZ ANSWERS

1. Before 1935, what effect had plant diseases and insects had on Kochen's rice crop?
   Very little. (Hardly any. Relatively little.)

2. What was the source of the insect which caused the damage to Kochen's rice crop?
   Thailand

3. What method of control was used to combat the insect?
   ( ) DDT
   ( ) Powerful insecticides
   ( ) Strict plant quarantine
   (X) Not stated

4. What is the name of the insect responsible for the agricultural catastrophe in 1935 in Kochen?
   Rice stem borer

5. What percentage of the 1935 rice crop was destroyed?
   Approximately 75%. (About 75%. Roughly 75%.)

6. Describe the conditions which made Kochen a "sitting duck" for the 1935 trouble.
   Relatively cool summer, below-average rainfall, no strict plant-quarantine regulations, no appropriate insecticides available.

Foreign Relations

READING PREPARATION

The subject of this lecture is an overview of Kochen's foreign policy. The lecturer reminds us that the prime minister is Det Sowatsam, and his brother Nek is the minister of foreign affairs. He says that the brothers are quite close, and have a harmonious working relationship in government matters.

He adds that Kochen and its neighbors have gotten along well over the years. There have been some minor incidents throughout history, but nothing of any great consequence. Of necessity Kochen has had to have harmonious international relations because of its landlocked position and need for seaports from which to export its main product, rice.

Much of the credit for the amicable relations over the past two decades goes to Nek Sowatsam, the foreign minister. It is noted that he is an extremely charming and personable diplomat with great talent. He speaks Thai, English, French, and Vietnamese fluently. Further, he has relatives in Thailand, Laos, and Vietnam. The lecturer notes that having relatives in these countries is an asset for diplomatic purposes, but denies suggesting that Nek pulls family strings to achieve his purposes.

Flexible neutrality is the term the lecturer uses to describe Kochen's foreign policy. For a long time, Kochen has been an independent state, and it is obvious that the bordering countries have benefited from Kochen's acting as a buffer state. Because of this position, Kochen has been a haven for political refugees from neighboring states. The lecturer says that a kind of tacit agreement seems to exist among Kochen's neighbors that Kochen is a place where those in political trouble can escape to. In return for this, any taxes levied against Kochen's shipments of rice have been quietly paid without complaint.

DICTATION

1. _____   1. _____

2. _____   2. _____

3. _____   3. _____

4. _____   4. _____

5. _____   5. _____

6. _____   6. _____

7. _____   7. _____

8. _____   8. _____

9. _____   9. _____

10. _____   10. _____

11. _____   11. _____

12. _____   12. _____

13. _____   13. _____

14. _____   14. _____

15. _____   15. _____

16. _____   16. _____

17. _____   17. _____

18. _____   18. _____

19. _____   19. _____

20. _____   20. _____

21. _____   21. _____

22. _____   22. _____

23. _____   23. _____

24. _____   24. _____

25. _____   25. _____

Number correct _____

AUDING PROMPT A

T̸ø̸d̸a̸y̸/I̸'d̸ l̸i̸k̸e̸ t̸ø̸ touch on Kochen's foreign policy, b̸u̸t̸ only in t̸h̸e̸ very broadest terms. L̸e̸t̸ m̸e̸ refresh your memory b̸y̸ s̸a̸y̸i̸n̸g̸ t̸h̸a̸t̸ t̸h̸e̸ prime minister is Det Sowatsam a̸n̸d̸ his brother Nek is t̸h̸e̸ minister of foreign affairs. Y̸ø̸u̸ w̸i̸l̸l̸ recall t̸h̸a̸t̸ these r̸ø̸y̸a̸l̸ brothers are very close, which makes for a̸ harmonious working relationship insofar as foreign policy matters are concerned.

Kochen has gotten along well with i̸t̸s̸ neighbors over the years. N̸ø̸w̸, t̸h̸i̸s̸ i̸s̸ not to say t̸h̸a̸t̸ there haven't been minor incidents between Kochen and t̸h̸e̸ bordering countries f̸r̸ø̸m̸ t̸i̸m̸e̸ t̸ø̸ t̸i̸m̸e̸, but c̸e̸r̸t̸a̸i̸n̸l̸y̸ nothing of a̸n̸y̸ significance. One could argue t̸h̸a̸t̸ harmonious relations have been a necessity for Kochen for t̸h̸e̸ v̸e̸r̸y̸ obvious reason t̸h̸a̸t̸ Kochen is landlocked and needs seaports to export i̸t̸s̸ principal product, rice, along with i̸t̸s̸ minor exports.

A̸ great deal of credit for t̸h̸e̸ amicable relations over t̸h̸e̸ past twenty years ø̸r̸ s̸ø̸ i̸s̸ due to Nek Sowatsam, t̸h̸e̸ minister of foreign affairs. Nek is not only a very able diplomat, but h̸e̸ i̸s̸ also a̸n̸ extremely charming a̸n̸d̸ personable i̸n̸d̸i̸v̸i̸d̸u̸a̸l̸. He speaks fluent French, English, Thai, a̸n̸d̸ Vietnamese. Ø̸n̸ t̸ø̸p̸ ø̸f̸ t̸h̸i̸s̸, he has relatives in Thailand, Laos, a̸n̸d̸ Vietnam. While I don't mean to suggest t̸h̸a̸t̸ he pulls family strings to achieve his purposes, having relatives in these countries is certainly not a hindrance.

Kochen's foreign policy m̸i̸g̸h̸t̸ b̸e̸ characterized as "flexible neutrality." Kochen has been a̸n̸ independent state for a̸ considerable length of time, a̸n̸d̸ it is apparent t̸h̸a̸t̸ t̸h̸e̸ surrounding countries—t̸h̸ø̸s̸e̸ that border Kochen—have benefited by Kochen's acting as a s̸ø̸r̸t̸ ø̸f̸ buffer s̸t̸a̸t̸e̸. As a result, Kochen has been, from time to time, a̸ haven for political refugees ø̸f̸ ø̸n̸e̸ k̸i̸n̸d̸ ø̸r̸ a̸n̸ø̸t̸h̸e̸r̸. T̸h̸e̸r̸e̸ seems to be tacit agreement among t̸h̸e̸ neighboring countries that Kochen is a̸ place where political misfits c̸a̸n̸ escape t̸ø̸. On its part, Kochen has quietly paid taxes levied on its rice shipments without undue complaint. T̸h̸a̸t̸'s̸ a̸l̸l̸ I̸ h̸a̸v̸e̸ t̸i̸m̸e̸ f̸ø̸r̸.

AUDING PROMPT B

_____ _____ _____ _____ touch on Kochen's foreign policy, _____ only in _____ very broadest terms. _____ _____ refresh your memory _____ _____ _____ _____ prime minister is Det Sowatsam _____ his brother Nek is _____ minister of foreign affairs. _____ _____ recall _____ these _____ brothers are very close, which makes for _____ harmonious working relationship insofar as foreign policy matters are concerned.

Kochen has gotten along well with _____ neighbors over the years. _____, _____ _____ not to say _____ there haven't been minor incidents between Kochen and _____ bordering countries _____ _____ _____ _____, but _____ nothing of _____ significance. One could argue _____ harmonious relations have been a necessity for Kochen for _____ _____ obvious reason _____ Kochen is landlocked and needs seaports to export _____ principal product, rice, along with _____ minor exports.

_____ great deal of credit for _____ amicable relations over _____ past twenty years _____ _____ _____ due to Nek Sowatsam, _____ minister of foreign affairs. Nek is not only a very able diplomat, but _____ _____ also _____ extremely charming _____ personable _____. He speaks fluent French, English, Thai, _____ Vietnamese. _____ _____ _____ _____, he has relatives in Thailand, Laos, _____ Vietnam. While I don't mean to suggest _____ he pulls family strings to achieve his purposes, having relatives in these countries is _____ not a hindrance.

Kochen's foreign policy _____ _____ characterized as "flexible neutrality." Kochen has been _____ independent state for _____ considerable length of time, _____ it is apparent _____ _____ surrounding countries—_____ that border Kochen—have benefited by Kochen's acting as _____ _____ _____ buffer _____. As a result, Kochen has been, from time to time, _____ haven for political refugees _____ _____ _____ _____ _____. _____ seems to be tacit agreement among _____ neighboring countries that Kochen is _____ place where political misfits _____ escape _____. On its part, Kochen has quietly paid taxes levied on its rice shipments without undue complaint. _____ _____ _____ _____ _____ _____.

AUDING PROMPT C

—— touch on —— Kochen's —— foreign —— policy —— only —— broadest —— terms ——. —— prime minister —— Det Sowatsam —— brother —— Nek —— minister —— foreign —— affairs ——. —— brothers —— very —— close —— makes —— for —— harmonious —— working —— relationship —— foreign —— policy —— matters ——.

—— Kochen —— gotten —— along —— well —— with —— neighbors —— over —— years ——. —— not to say —— haven't —— been —— incidents —— between —— Kochen —— bordering —— countries —— nothing —— of —— significance ——. —— could —— argue —— harmonious —— relations —— necessity —— Kochen —— landlocked —— needs —— seaports —— export —— rice —— minor —— exports ——.

—— credit —— for —— amicable —— relations —— past —— twenty —— years —— due to —— Nek Sowatsam —— minister —— foreign —— affairs ——. —— Nek —— able —— diplomat —— extremely —— charming —— personable ——. —— speaks —— fluent —— French —— English —— Thai —— Vietnamese ——. —— has —— relatives —— in —— Thailand —— Laos —— Vietnam ——. —— don't —— mean —— suggest —— pulls —— family strings —— achieve —— purposes —— having —— relatives —— in —— these —— countries —— not —— hindrance ——.

—— Kochen's —— foreign —— policy —— characterized —— "flexible neutrality'' ——. —— Kochen —— independent —— state —— considerable —— time —— apparent —— surrounding —— countries —— benefited —— Kochen's —— acting —— buffer ——. —— Kochen —— time to time —— haven —— political —— refugees ——. —— tacit —— agreement —— among —— neighboring —— countries —— Kochen —— place —— political —— misfits —— escape to ——. ——Kochen —— quietly —— paid —— taxes —— levied —— on —— rice —— shipments —— without —— undue —— complaint ——.

NOTES

Foreign policy—broad terms

    PM—Det S

                }   Bros. work well together

    Min of For Aff.—Nek S

Kochen gotten along OK w/ neighbors

    Some minor incidents; nothing serious

Kochen—landlocked, *must* get along w/ neighbors

      —needs seaports for export

    Much credit goes to Nek S—good relations past 20 yrs.

      Able diplomat, charming, personable

      Spks fluent French, Eng., Thai, Vietnamese

      Has relatives in Thailand, Laos, V-N. Family connections help him.

    Foreign policy—"flexible neutrality"

      Kochen—independent long time

        Bordering countries have benefited from K's buffer role

        Haven for political refugees

        Neighboring countries agree Kochen OK for pol. refugees

    Kochen has pd. taxes on its rice shipments w/o undue complaining

YOUR NOTES

QUIZ

1. What is the name of the Kochenese minister of foreign affairs?

2. How would you describe the working relationship between the prime minister and the minister of foreign affairs of Kochen?

3. Why does the lecturer say that it is necessary for Kochen to get along with its neighbors?

4. The lecturer mentioned several personal qualities of the Kochenese minister of foreign affairs which particularly suit him for his job. What are these?

5. What terms did the lecturer use to characterize Kochen's foreign policy?

6. What is Kochen's attitude toward levies on its rice?

QUIZ ANSWERS

1. What is the name of the Kochenese minister of foreign affairs?
   Nek Sowatsam

2. How would you describe the working relationship between the prime minister and the minister of foreign affairs of Kochen?
   Harmonious (Amicable, Good, Excellent, etc.)

3. Why does the lecturer say that it is necessary for Kochen to get along with its neighbors?
   Kochen is landlocked and must ship its rice through neighboring countries.

4. The lecturer mentioned several personal qualities of the Kochenese minister of foreign affairs which particularly suit him for his job. What are these?
   Able diplomat, charming, personable, fluent speaker of French, English, Thai, Vietnamese.

5. What terms did the lecturer use to characterize Kochen's foreign policy?
   Flexible neutrality

6. What is Kochen's attitude toward levies on its rice?
   It pays them without complaining too much.

Sports and Games

READING PREPARATION

The lecturer reminds the listener that Queen Pingpum is a sports enthusiast. He says that this enthusiasm is not restricted to the queen and her coterie of friends, and that sports and games of many different kinds are enjoyed throughout Kochen. Because Kochen is not an affluent country, most of the sports and games do not require much equipment. He notes that the only major cash outlay for recreational activities was the money spent to build the sports arena, which is in the center of Norkhan.

The more popular sports, the lecturer says, include badminton; tennis—even though there aren't too many courts; *rawtak,* a type of kick-ball played with a hollow rattan ball that is very popular in such places as Hong Kong, the Philippines, Malaysia, Thailand, and Burma; and the more common track and field events in the high schools and Popupat University.

The most important sport is soccer or, as it is also known, football. The lecturer says that the use of the two words—*soccer* and *football*—causes some confusion among Americans, for whom football is an entirely different game. He mentions that the shoe is on the other foot when Asians come to America and hear about football. The official name is association football, but he suggests that for the purposes of his lecture, soccer is sufficient. Yearly, in January, the Kochenese host an invitational soccer meet lasting three days. The entire three days are consumed with nothing but soccer. Teams come from Burma, Vietnam, Laos, Singapore, the Philippines, Thailand, Malaysia and Indonesia. It seems to be a very festive occasion and a great deal of pomp and ceremony goes along with it. Evidently this is one of the major events of the year and is worth seeing. The meet is opened by Her Majesty the Queen, and important government dignitaries and officials come from the various countries.

DICTATION

1. _____
2. _____
3. _____
4. _____
5. _____
6. _____
7. _____
8. _____
9. _____
10. _____
11. _____
12. _____
13. _____
14. _____
15. _____
16. _____
17. _____
18. _____
19. _____
20. _____
21. _____

1. _____
2. _____
3. _____
4. _____
5. _____
6. _____
7. _____
8. _____
9. _____
10. _____
11. _____
12. _____
13. _____
14. _____
15. _____
16. _____
17. _____
18. _____
19. _____
20. _____
21. _____

22. _____   22. _____

23. _____   23. _____

24. _____   24. _____

25. _____   25. _____

Number correct _____

AUDING PROMPT A

I mentioned some time ago that Queen Pingpum was a sports enthusiast. This enthusiasm for sports is certainly not restricted to her and her coterie of friends. Sports and games of a variety of sorts are enjoyed throughout the kingdom. Kochen is not an affluent country, so most of the sports and games are those which can be played with a minimum of equipment. In fact, the only major outlay of cash for recreational activities was the money which went into the sports arena in the heart of Norkhan.

Some of the more popular sports include badminton, tennis—although there aren't too many courts; and a type of kick-ball called *rawtak,* played with a hollow rattan ball, popular all over the East including Hong Kong, the Philippines, Malaysia, Thailand, and Burma. We also find the usual track and field events in the high schools and at the university.

The most important sport by far is soccer or, as it is known more commonly, football. Incidentally, this use of the two words causes confusion among Americans, for whom football is an entirely different game. By the same token, the Kochenese and other Asians are also confused when they come to America and hear about football. I believe the official name is association football, or something like that. Let's call it soccer and not worry about it. Every year in January, the Kochenese hold an invitational soccer meet which lasts three days. It's nothing but soccer, soccer, soccer for three whole days. Teams come from Burma, Vietnam, Laos, Singapore, the Philippines, Thailand. Where else? Oh, yes, Malaysia and Indonesia. There is a great deal of pomp and ceremony connected with this invitational meet and the whole thing is a very festive occasion. It's really something to see. Queen Pingpum always opens the event, and often important government dignitaries come from the various countries.

AUDING PROMPT B

_____ mentioned _____ _____ _____ _____ Queen Pingpum was a sports enthusiast. _____ enthusiasm for sports _____ _____ not restricted to her _____ _____ coterie of friends. Sports and games of a variety of sorts _____ enjoyed throughout _____ kingdom. Kochen _____ not _____ affluent country, _____ most of _____ sports and games _____ those which can be played with _____ minimum _____ equipment. _____ _____, _____ only major outlay of cash for recreational activities _____ _____ _____ _____ went into _____ sports arena in _____ _____ _____ Norkhan.

_____ _____ _____ more popular sports include badminton; tennis—_____ _____ aren't _____ many courts; _____ _____ type of kick-ball called *rawtak,* played with _____ hollow rattan ball, popular all over _____ East including Hong Kong, _____ Philippines, Malaysia, Thailand, _____ Burma. _____ also find _____ usual track and field events in _____ high schools and _____ _____ university.

_____ most important sport _____ _____ is soccer or, _____ _____ _____ _____ _____ _____, football. _____, _____ use of the two words causes confusion among Americans, for whom football is _____ _____ different game. By _____ same token, _____ Kochenese and other Asians _____ also confused when _____ come to America and hear about football. _____ _____ _____ official name is association football, _____ _____ _____ _____. Let's call it soccer _____ _____ _____ _____ _____. Every year in January, the Kochenese hold _____ invitational soccer meet _____ _____ three days. _____ nothing but soccer, _____, _____ for three _____ days. Teams come from Burma, Vietnam, Laos, Singapore, _____ Philippines, Thailand. _____ _____? _____, _____, Malaysia and Indonesia. _____ _____ _____ great deal of pomp _____ ceremony connected with this invitational meet and _____ _____ _____ is _____ very festive occasion. _____ really something to see. Queen Pingpum always opens _____ event, and often important government dignitaries come from _____ various countries.

AUDING PROMPT C

_____ mentioned _____ Queen Pingpum _____ sports _____ enthusiast _____. _____ enthusiasm _____ sports _____ not _____ restricted _____ her _____ coterie _____ friends _____. _____ sports _____ games _____ variety _____ of _____ sorts _____ enjoyed _____ throughout _____ kingdom _____. _____ Kochen _____ not _____ affluent _____ country _____ most _____ sports _____ games _____ those _____ played _____ minimum _____ equipment _____. _____ major _____ outlay _____ cash _____ recreational _____ activities _____ into _____ sports _____ arena _____ Norkhan _____.

_____ popular _____ sports _____ badminton _____ tennis _____ _rawtak_ _____ played _____ East _____ Hong Kong _____ Philippines _____ Malaysia _____ Thailand _____ Burma _____. _____ usual _____ track _____ field _____ events _____ high schools _____ university _____.

_____ most _____ important _____ sport _____ soccer _____ football _____. _____ use _____ two _____ words _____ causes _____ confusion _____ Americans _____ for _____ whom _____ football _____ different _____ game _____. _____ Kochenese _____ Asians _____ also _____ confused _____ come _____ America _____ hear _____ about _____ football _____. _____ official _____ name _____ association _____ football _____. _____ every _____ January _____ Kochenese _____ hold _____ invitational _____ soccer _____ meet _____ three _____ days _____. _____ soccer _____ three _____ days _____. _____ teams _____ from _____ Burma _____ Vietnam _____ Laos _____ Singapore _____ Philippines _____ Thailand. _____ Malaysia _____ Indonesia _____. _____ great _____ pomp _____ ceremony _____ connected _____ invitational _____ meet _____ festive _____ occasion _____. _____ something _____ see _____. _____ Queen Pingpum _____ opens _____ event _____ government _____ dignitaries _____ come _____ from _____ various _____ countries _____.

NOTES

Queen Pingpum—sports enthusiast

Sports & games enjoyed throughout kingdom

Prefer sports which aren't expensive, don't use much equipment

Sports arena in Norkhan = most costly item

Popular sports

badminton, tennis (few courts), *rawtak* (hollow rattan ball, kick-ball) played all

over East

Track & field @ high schools & univ.

Soccer—most imp. (also called football)

America—football = different game, so some confusion of terms football–

soccer

Official name = assoc. football

January—yearly—3-day invitational soccer meet

Teams: Burma, V-N, Laos, Sing., Phil., Thailand, Malaysia, Indonesia

Much pomp/ceremony—very festive

Queen opens meet, big shots from other countries present

YOUR NOTES

QUIZ

1. What is the official name for soccer?

2. What is the most important sporting event in Kochen? When is it held and how long does it last?

3. What sports other than soccer did the lecturer cite as being popular?

4. Describe briefly the sporting event in 2, above.

QUIZ ANSWERS

1. What is the official name for soccer?
   Association football.

2. What is the most important sporting event in Kochen? When is it held and
   how long does it last?
   The three-day invitational soccer meet in January.

3. What sports other than soccer did the lecturer cite as being popular?
   Tennis, badminton, *rawtak*. (Track and field events might be included in
   your answer.)

4. Describe briefly the sporting event in 2, above.
   This is a very colorful and festive occasion at which both Kochenese and
   other countries' dignitaries are in attendance.

Kochenese Ceremonies

READING PREPARATION

According to the lecturer, two of the most expensive happenings in a Kochenese's life are his marriage and his funeral. Getting married or buried in many other cultures can be expensive too, but the lecturer feels that the Kochenese spend far more than others on these ceremonies. He further says that considering economics, one could argue that this money might be spent in better ways, but after all, what is important in Kochenese terms is not necessarily important to others.

The Kochenese still follow old customs. For example, they pay a bride-price, a sum of money which can be quite large. Wealthy families, the lecturer notes, may pay as much as $10,000 or more. As one moves down the economic and social scale, the bride-price becomes smaller, but it still represents a fair amount of money for the particular family. This bride-price is normally paid in cash or an equivalent amount of gold and jewelry. On occasion, the lecturer continues, other goods are used in lieu of money. The lecturer says that according to his sources of information there is no trend away from this custom, although it is dying out in other cultures fairly rapidly.

The other major expense in the life of a Kochenese is his funeral. The lecturer notes that Kochenese Christians face a dilemma because a Christian service and burial come to much less money than a Buddhist cremation and all its ceremonial aspects. However, because of strong cultural pressures, the Kochenese feel they must have a show of splendor at funerals. So, certain facets of Buddhism are present in Christian funerals. This has no connection with religion, the lecturer adds, but rather a direct connection with the important concept of face, something which is found throughout the East.

DICTATION

1. _____	1. _____
2. _____	2. _____
3. _____	3. _____
4. _____	4. _____
5. _____	5. _____
6. _____	6. _____
7. _____	7. _____
8. _____	8. _____
9. _____	9. _____
10. _____	10. _____
11. _____	11. _____
12. _____	12. _____
13. _____	13. _____
14. _____	14. _____
15. _____	15. _____
16. _____	16. _____
17. _____	17. _____
18. _____	18. _____
19. _____	19. _____
20. _____	20. _____
21. _____	21. _____

22. _____   22. _____

23. _____   23. _____

24. _____   24. _____

25. _____   25. _____

Number correct _____

AUDING PROMPT A

Two of the most costly events in the life of a Kochenese are his marriage and his funeral. One hears of the high cost of living, but in Kochen one would also have to talk about the high cost of dying! While I freely admit that getting married or buried can be expensive in many other cultures, I think that the Kochenese take the cake for spending money on these two ceremonies. From an economic standpoint, it is easy to argue that this money could be better spent in other ways, but then what is important to a Kochenese is not necessarily important to you and me.

The Kochenese engage in the old practice of paying a bride-price, and this can amount to a fair piece of change. For example, in wealthy families a bride-price in the neighborhood of $10,000 or more is not unheard of. Naturally, the lower one goes on the economic and social scale, the smaller the bride-price becomes. However, it still represents a sizable sum of money for the particular family concerned. The bride-price is usually paid in cash or an equivalent amount in gold and precious stones. Sometimes, though, other goods are used instead of money. The latest information which I have indicates that there is no trend away from this custom, although in other cultures, I understand that it is dying out at a fairly rapid rate.

As I indicated before, the other big expense in the life of a Kochenese concerns death. I might add here that Kochenese Christians face something of a dilemma in that a Christian service and burial are considerably cheaper than a Buddhist cremation with all the attendant ceremonies. Yet a Kochenese is a Kochenese, and a big show is a cultural requirement at the time of death. Thus, we see some carry-over from Buddhist practices in the funerals of Kochenese Christians. This has nothing to do with religion per se, but has a lot to do with face—an important concept in the countries and regions of the East.

AUDING PROMPT B

Two _____ _____ most costly events in _____ life of _____ Kochenese are _____ marriage and _____ funeral. One hears of _____ high cost of living, _____ in Kochen one would _____ have to talk about _____ high cost of dying! _____ I freely admit _____ getting married or buried can be expensive in many _____ cultures, I think _____ _____ Kochenese take the cake for spending money on these _____ ceremonies. From _____ economic standpoint, _____ _____ easy to argue _____ this money could be better spent _____ _____ _____, but _____ what is important to _____ Kochenese is not necessarily important to you and me.

_____ Kochenese engage in _____ old practice of paying _____ bride-price, _____ this can amount to _____ _____ piece of change. _____ _____, in wealthy families a bride-price _____ _____ _____ of $10,000 or more is not unheard of.

_____, the lower one goes on the economic and social scale, the smaller _____ bride-price becomes. However, _____ still represents _____ sizable sum _____ _____ for _____ particular family _____. _____ bride-price _____ usually paid in cash or _____ equivalent amount in gold and precious stones. Sometimes, _____, other goods _____ used instead of money. _____ latest information _____ I have indicates _____ there is no trend away from this custom, although in other cultures, I understand _____ it is dying _____ at _____ fairly rapid rate.

_____ _____ _____ _____, _____ other big expense in _____ life of _____ Kochenese concerns death. _____ _____ _____ _____ _____ Kochenese Christians face _____ _____ a dilemma in that a Christian service and burial _____ considerably cheaper than _____ Buddhist cremation with _____ _____ attendant ceremonies. _____ a Kochenese is a Kochenese, _____ _____ big show is _____ cultural requirement at _____ time of death. Thus, _____ _____ some carry-over from Buddhist practices in _____ funerals of Kochenese Christians. _____ _____ nothing to do with religion per se, but _____ a lot to do with face—_____ important concept in _____ countries and regions of _____ East.

AUDING PROMPT C

—— two —— most —— costly —— events —— life —— Kochenese —— marriage —— funeral ——. —— one —— hears —— cost —— living —— Kochen —— talk —— about —— cost —— dying ——. —— admit —— getting —— married —— buried —— expensive —— many —— cultures —— Kochenese —— take —— cake —— spending —— money —— these —— ceremonies ——. —— from —— economic —— standpoint —— easy —— argue —— money —— better —— spent —— but —— what —— important —— to —— Kochenese —— not —— necessarily —— important —— you —— me ——.

—— Kochenese —— engage —— practice —— paying —— bride-price ——. —— wealthy —— families —— bride-price —— $10,000 —— or —— more —— not —— unheard —— of ——. —— lower —— on —— economic —— social —— scale —— smaller —— bride-price —— becomes ——. —— still —— represents —— sizable —— sum —— for —— particular —— family ——. —— bride-price —— usually —— paid —— cash —— equivalent —— amount —— gold —— precious stones ——. —— sometimes —— goods —— used —— instead —— money ——. —— latest —— information —— indicates —— no —— trend —— away —— from —— custom —— other —— cultures —— dying —— fairly —— rapid —— rate ——.

—— other —— big —— expense —— life —— of —— Kochenese —— death ——. —— Kochenese —— Christians —— face —— dilemma —— Christian —— service —— burial —— considerably —— cheaper —— than —— Buddhist —— cremation —— with —— attendant —— ceremonies ——. —— Kochenese —— is —— Kochenese —— big —— show —— cultural

—— requirement —— time —— of —— death ——. —— some —— carry-over —— Buddhist —— practices —— funerals —— Kochenese —— Chris-tians ——. —— nothing —— to —— do —— with —— religion —— per se —— lot —— to do —— with —— face —— important —— concept —— in —— countries —— regions —— East ——.

NOTES

Marriage & funeral = 2 most costly items in Kochenese life

Spend lot of money, more than other cultures

Pay bride-price

Wealthy families—±$10,000 possible

Lower on econ/soc scale, not so much—*but* still represents sizable amt

Pd in cash or gold & precious stones, sometimes other goods used

No trend away from custom; other cultures, yes—fairly rapidly

Death

K. Christians face dilemma: burial/service cheaper than Buddhist cremation

But putting on dog is culturally imp. So, some Buddhist practices seen in Chr.

funerals. No relation to religion—but tied in w/ face (imp. in East)

YOUR NOTES

QUIZ

1. Which is the most expensive item in the life of a Kochenese?
   ( ) Marriage
   ( ) Funeral
   ( ) Marriage and funeral are equal
   ( ) Lecturer didn't specify

2. How did the lecturer feel about the relative amount of money the Kochenese spend for marriage and funeral ceremonies compared with other cultures?
   ( ) About the same
   ( ) Much more
   ( ) A little more
   ( ) Much less
   ( ) A little less

3. What means of payment may a Kochenese use to pay his bride-price?

4. Compare the viability of the bride-price custom in Kochenese culture with other cultures.

5. Explain the dilemma Kochenese Christians face concerning funeral practices.

QUIZ ANSWERS

1. Which is the most expensive item in the life of a Kochenese?
   ( ) Marriage
   ( ) Funeral
   ( ) Marriage and funeral are equal
   (X) Lecturer didn't specify

2. How did the lecturer feel about the relative amount of money the Kochenese spend for marriage and funeral ceremonies compared with other cultures?
   ( ) About the same
   (X) Much more
   ( ) A little more
   ( ) Much less
   ( ) A little less

3. What means of payment may a Kochenese use to pay his bride-price?
   Cash, equivalent amount in gold and precious stones, other goods of an equivalent amount.

4. Compare the viability of the bride-price custom in Kochenese culture with other cultures.
   In Kochen the custom is very much alive, but it is dying out in other cultures.

5. Explain the dilemma Kochenese Christians face concerning funeral practices.
   Impressive funerals are important in Kochenese culture. However, Christians have relatively cheap funerals compared with Buddhist cremations. Thus, to maintain face, Christians have borrowed some aspects of the Buddhist ceremonies.

Foreign Investment

READING PREPARATION

The lecturer points out that within recent years, interest on the part of foreigners has been growing in the investment possibilities in Kochen. What, he asks, does Kochen have to offer potential investors? An agricultural country, Kochen has few or no natural resources such as iron ore, coal, and oil. What Kochen does have is an adequate supply of cheap labor. As a result, one would expect that small assembly plants would be found which could use Kochen's reasonably well-educated people as a labor force.

The Burex Watch Company of New York was the first company to establish a plant in Kochen. It took some five years of long, drawn-out negotiations before an agreement was reached because, for example, the Kochenese didn't want a huge factory in the middle of Norkhan polluting the atmosphere. According to the lecturer, Nup Sowatsam, the minister of commerce—who happens to be a cousin of the queen—wanted to be very sure that the factory would harmonize with the environment of Norkhan. Such things as division of profits had to be worked out. The Burex people received a 25-year lease for their factory with an option to extend the lease another 25 years if everything was satisfactory. The lecturer notes that such items as working conditions, vacation time and pay, bonuses, and so forth were carefully arranged in what probably seemed unending conferences to the Burex officials who hadn't had experience in doing business in Kochen. But everything turned out all right in the end. There are 200 employes in the factory, most of them women. It has been a profitable venture, according to the lecturer.

This first assembly plant paved the way for other investors because all the groundwork had been done. The Fujinomoto Trading Company of Japan was the next company to establish a small factory in Kochen. Following the example set by the Burex Watch Company, they established a small plant to assemble transistor radios.

DICTATION

1. _____   1. _____

2. _____   2. _____

3. _____   3. _____

4. _____   4. _____

5. _____   5. _____

6. _____   6. _____

7. _____   7. _____

8. _____   8. _____

9. _____   9. _____

10. _____   10. _____

11. _____   11. _____

12. _____   12. _____

13. _____   13. _____

14. _____   14. _____

15. _____   15. _____

16. _____   16. _____

17. _____   17. _____

18. _____   18. _____

19. _____   19. _____

20. _____   20. _____

21. _____   21. _____

22. _____   22. _____

23. _____   23. _____

24. _____   24. _____

25. _____   25. _____

Number correct _____

AUDING PROMPT A

Within the past few years, interest has been growing in the possibilities of foreign investment in Kochen. In this connection, it is reasonable to ask what Kochen has to offer potential investors. Remember that Kochen has an agricultural economy, and there are no natural resources such as iron ore, coal, and oil to speak of. What Kochen does have is a good supply of relatively cheap labor. Consequently, we would expect to find small assembly plants which could utilize Kochen's reasonably well-educated people as a labor force.

The first company to establish a plant in Kochen was the Burex Watch Company of New York. The negotiations were extremely tedious, lasting some five years before agreement was reached. The Kochenese didn't want a big, ugly factory belching smoke smack dab in the heart of Norkhan. The minister of commerce, Nup Sowatsam—another member of the ruling family, in this case a cousin of the queen—wanted to make doubly sure that the factory wouldn't clash with Norkhan's feeling and character. Further, the division of profits had to be agreed upon. Land for the factory was leased to the Burex people for 25 years with an option for an extension of another 25 if both parties agreed. Such things as working conditions, vacation time and pay, and bonuses were all hammered out in what must have seemed interminable conferences to the Burex people, who were not used to doing business Kochenese style. However, the result was that everybody was happy with the agreements. The factory employs 200 Kochenese, mostly women, and has proved to be profitable for all concerned.

The successful establishment of the Burex assembly plant paved the way for other investors in that a model had been set up which could be emulated or improved on. The next company to approach the Kochenese was the Fujinomoto Trading Company of Japan. They set up a transistor radio assembly plant with arrangements modeled after those established by the Burex Company.

AUDING PROMPT B

Within _____ past few years, interest _____ _____ growing in _____ possibilities of foreign investment in Kochen. _____ _____ _____, _____ _____ reasonable to ask what Kochen has to offer potential investors. _____ _____ Kochen has _____ agricultural economy, and _____ _____ no natural resources such as iron ore, coal, and oil to speak of. _____ Kochen does have _____ _____ good supply of relatively cheap labor. Consequently, _____ _____ expect to find small assembly plants which could utilize Kochen's reasonably well-educated people as _____ labor _____.

_____ first company to establish a plant in Kochen was _____ Burex Watch Company of New York. _____ negotiations were extremely tedious, lasting some five years before agreement _____ reached. _____ Kochenese didn't want

_____ big, ugly factory belching smoke smack dab in _____ heart of Norkhan. _____ minister of commerce, Nup Sowatsam—_____ _____ _____ _____ _____ _____, _____ _____ _____ _____ cousin of the queen— wanted to make doubly sure _____ _____ factory wouldn't clash with Norkhan's feeling and character. Further, _____ division of profits had to be agreed upon. Land for _____ factory _____ leased to _____ Burex _____ for 25 years with _____ option for _____ extension of _____ 25 if both parties agreed. _____ _____ _____ working conditions, vacation time and pay, and bonuses were all hammered out in what must have seemed interminable conferences to _____ Burex _____, _____ _____ not used to doing business Kochenese style. However, _____ result _____ _____ everybody was happy with _____ agreements. _____ factory employs 200 Kochenese, mostly women, _____ has proved to be profitable for all _____.

_____ successful establishment of _____ Burex assembly plant paved _____ way for other investors in that _____ model had been set up which could be emulated or improved on. _____ next company to approach _____ Kochenese was _____ Fujinomoto Trading Company of Japan. They set up _____ transistor radio assembly plant with arrangements modeled after those established by _____ Burex _____.

AUDING PROMPT C

—— past —— few —— years —— interest —— growing —— foreign —— investment —— Kochen ——. —— reasonable —— ask —— what —— Kochen —— offer —— potential —— investors ——. —— Kochen —— agricultural —— economy —— no —— natural —— resources —— iron ore —— coal —— oil ——. —— Kochen —— good —— supply —— relatively —— cheap —— labor ——. —— expect —— find —— small —— assembly —— plants —— utilize —— reasonably —— well-educated —— people —— labor ——.

—— first —— company —— establish —— plant —— Kochen —— Burex Watch Company ——. —— negotiations —— tedious —— lasting —— five —— years —— before —— agreement ——. —— Kochenese —— didn't —— want —— big —— ugly —— factory —— belching —— smoke —— heart —— Norkhan ——. —— Minister of Commerce —— Nup Sowatsam —— cousin —— queen —— wanted —— make —— doubly —— sure —— factory —— wouldn't —— clash —— with —— Norkhan's —— feeling —— character ——. —— division —— profits —— agreed —— upon ——. —— land —— for —— factory —— leased —— Burex —— 25 years —— option —— extension —— 25 —— if —— both —— parties —— agreed ——. —— working —— conditions —— vacation —— time —— pay —— bonuses —— hammered out —— what —— must —— have —— seemed —— interminable —— conferences —— to —— Burex —— not —— used —— doing ——business —— Kochenese —— style ——. —— result —— everybody —— happy

——. —— factory —— employs —— 200 —— mostly —— women —— proved —— profitable ——.

—— successful —— establishment —— Burex —— assembly —— plant —— paved —— way —— other —— investors —— model —— set up —— could —— be —— emulated ——. —— next —— company —— approach —— Kochenese —— Fujinomoto Trading Company —— Japan ——. —— set up —— transistor —— radio —— assembly —— plant —— arrangements —— modeled —— after —— Burex ——.

NOTES

Foreign investment—growing interest

   Kochen = agric economy, few natural resources available

   Good supply of relatively cheap labor; thus small assembly plants make sense

1st Company

   Burex Watch Co., NY

      Negotiations tedious, took 5 yrs

   Nup Sowatsam (queen's cousin) min of comm—wanted no clashes

      w/ Norkhan's environment

   Land for factory—25 yr lease; 25 yr extension possible if mutually OK

   Long, drawn-out conferences needed to set wages, working hrs., etc.

   200 employes, mostly women

   Profitable

2nd Co

   Fujinomoto Trading Co—assemble transistor radios

   Followed Burex model

YOUR NOTES

QUIZ

1. What was the reasoning behind the establishment of small assembly plants in Kochen?

2. How would you characterize the negotiations between the Kochenese government and the first foreign company to establish a factory in Kochen?

3. What were the terms of the lease granted to the first company to operate in Kochen?

4. Kochen's minister of commerce had certain reservations and concerns before permitting establishment of factories in Norkhan. Describe.

5. What were the two companies which established the initial factories in Kochen?

QUIZ ANSWERS

1. What was the reasoning behind the establishment of small assembly plants in Kochen?

   Kochen has no natural resources, but does have a good supply of relatively cheap, reasonably well-educated labor.

2. How would you characterize the negotiations between the Kochenese government and the first foreign company to establish a factory in Kochen?

   Tedious (or) Long and drawn out (or) Seemingly interminable

3. What were the terms of the lease granted to the first foreign company to operate in Kochen?

   25 years with an option for another 25-year extension if mutually agreeable.

4. Kochen's minister of commerce had certain reservations and concerns before permitting establishment of factories in Norkhan. Describe.

   He wanted to make sure that any such factories didn't disturb or upset Norkhan's total environment.

5. What were the two companies which established the initial factories in Kochen?

   The Burex Watch Company and the Fujinomoto Trading Company.

Vocabulary Study

LECTURE 1 / OVERVIEW

Line 2 *a handful*—a small number; a few
Line 4 *globe*—the earth; the world
Line 23 *I'm getting a little ahead of myself*—talking about something ahead o
the time I had planned to talk about it

LECTURE 2 / CLIMATE

Line 1 *ties in with*—is related to
Line 13 *a handle*—a name
Line 20 *hits*—reaches
Line 23 *to take a jump*—to rise; to increase

LECTURE 3 / AGRICULTURE (I)

Line 2 *get my hands on*—to find; to obtain
Line 9 *to go into something*—to talk about it; to discuss it
Line 9 *to touch on something*—to talk about it; to discuss it, but not in depth
Line 17 *poured*—put in
Line 24 *The results speak for themselves*—the results are obvious; no explanation is necessary; the outcome is apparent

LECTURE 4 / AGRICULTURE (II)

Line 8 *along this line*—of this same type or kind
Line 25 *more than its share*—a large quantity; a great deal

283

LECTURE 5 / PRINCIPAL CITIES

Line 15   *what industry there is*—how much industry is present. (The implica-
tion is that there is very little industry, but what is present will be
found in Norkhan.)

LECTURE 6 / NORKHAN

Line 16   *caught on*—have become popular; have captured people's interest
Line 25   *catching on*—becoming popular; capturing people's interest

LECTURE 7 / THE MONARCHY

Line 17   *so to speak*—this is one way of saying something
Line 21   *in the driver's seat*—in command; in charge; leading

LECTURE 8 / QUEEN PINGPUM SOWATSAM

Line 1   *to put it mildly*—to understate something
Line 1   *quite a gal*—to be an interesting woman; to be impressive in some
way or another; to be accomplished in something. (The corresponding
expression for a male would be *quite a guy.*)
Line 2   *to put someone to shame*—to excel in something especially where ex-
cellence would not be expected (an elderly woman with great physical
strength and stamina, in our example)
Line 25   *take something in stride*—to take on a new task, especially a difficult
one, calmly and efficiently without a show of concern

LECTURE 9 / TRANSPORTATION

Line 21   *a bit of a headache*—a worry; something troublesome; something
bothersome

LECTURE 10 / POPULATION

Line 27   *and what have you*—*et cetera;* and so forth

LECTURE 11 / EDUCATION (I)

Line 12   *Stoneman bought the idea*—accepted the idea; agreed with the idea
Line 15   *crash courses*—concentrated, intensive teaching of a subject
Line 26   *going strong*—working particularly well

LECTURE 12 / EDUCATION (II)

Line 4   *I won't go into that*—I won't discuss it; I won't talk about it
Line 19   *rough*—approximate; not exact

LECTURE 13 / PUBLIC HEALTH (I)

Line 10   *wiped out*—eliminated; exterminated; done away with
Line 13   *age-old problem*—very old; continuing; a problem that won't go away
Line 18   *needless to say*—obviously; apparently; something which everyone knows

LECTURE 14 / PUBLIC HEALTH (II)

Line 1   *let's see*—an expression used by a person to gather his thoughts, to think about what he has been saying. (Also, *Let me see.*)
Line 9   *noodles*—intelligence; brains (also, *used their heads; used their beans*)
Line 10   *in keeping with*—appropriate to; suitable to
Line 16   *loosening up*—relaxing the restrictions
Line 23   *after all*—after everything has been considered

LECTURE 15 / RELIGION

Line 7   *hang on*—continue; exist
Line 18   *to gain a foothold*—to become established; to be permitted entry
Line 26   *follow suit*—to do likewise; to copy or imitate

LECTURE 16 / AGRICULTURAL DISASTER

Line 2   *bear in mind*—remember
Line 4   *rice is . . . king*—the most important crop; the number one crop

Line 16   *sitting duck*—extremely susceptible or vulnerable to something. (A duck sitting on the water is easy to shoot compared to one flying in the air.)

LECTURE 17 / FOREIGN RELATIONS

Line 15   *on top of this*—in addition to this
Line 17   *to pull family strings*—to take advantage of family influence; to use family influence and power

LECTURE 18 / SPORTS AND GAMES

Line 15   *by the same token*—for the same reason

LECTURE 19 / KOCHENESE CEREMONIES

Line 4   *take the cake*—to be the best at something; to be outstanding
Line 10   *fair piece of change*—reasonably large amount of money. (*Change* here refers to money.)

LECTURE 20 / FOREIGN INVESTMENT

Line 11   *smack dab*—exactly; directly
Line 11   *in the heart of*—in the center or middle of
Line 18   *hammered out*—discussed and agreed upon; carefully considered
Line 23   *paved the way*—made things smooth; set an example